Commodity Trading: Navigating Markets, Sustainability, and Innovation

Alex Thompson

Published by Side Hustle Success, 2023.

COMMODITY TRADING: NAVIGATING MARKETS, SUSTAINABILITY, AND INNOVATION

First edition. October 1, 2023.

ISBN: 979-8223559610

Written by Alex Thompson.

Also by Alex Thompson

Alex on Finance

Financial Freedom Roadmap - Achieving Early Retirement through the FIRE Movement

The Art of Strategic Innovation

Beyond Cash - The Evolution of Digital Payment Systems and the Future of Money

Preserving Wealth in Inflationary Times - Strategies for Protecting Your Financial Future

Standalone

Side Hustle Success: Unlocking Your Entrepreneurial Potential

Side Hustle Success: The Ultimate Guide to Passive and Financial Freedom

Mastering the Markets: Advanced Trading Strategies for Success and Ethical Trading Practices

Financial Fortitude

Mastering the Art of Upselling

The Financial Bullet Blueprint

Investing Demystified: A Beginner's Guide to Building Wealth in the Stock Market

Real Estate Riches: Building Wealth through Property Investment

How To Succeed as a Freelancer

Navigating Complex Waters: Advanced Strategies in Portfolio Management

Behavioral Finance and Investor Psychology

Leading with Empathy: Harnessing Emotional Intelligence for Effective Leadership

Financial Independence

Thriving Within Your Means: A Guide to Affordable Living

Algorithmic Trading: Navigating the Digital Frontier

Navigating Alternative Investments

Navigating the Behavioral Finance Landscape

Unlocking the Power of Derivatives

Mastering International Finance

Quantitative Finance and Risk Modeling

Sustainable and ESG Investing

Derivatives Dynamics: Navigating Risk and Innovation

Options Mastery: Navigating the Financial Frontier

Portfolio Mastery: Navigating the Financial Art and Science

Ethics in Hedge Funds: Navigating the Moral Compass of Finance

Structured Finance: Navigating Innovation, Sustainability and Ethics

Commodity Trading: Navigating Markets, Sustainability, and Innovation

Ethical Valuation: Navigating the Future of Startup Investments

Navigating Financial Risk: Strategies for a Dynamic World

Table of Contents

This book is dedicated to all those who seek to decipher the labyrinthine world of commodity trading, and to the trailblazing traders and innovators who will shape the markets of the future. May your journey be marked by curiosity, resilience, and a commitment to sustainable and responsible trading.

Chapter 1: Introduction to Commodity Trading

1. What Are Commodities?

Commodities are raw materials or primary agricultural products that can be bought and sold. They are typically standardized and interchangeable with other goods of the same type. Commodities can be categorized into several broad groups:

a. Agricultural Commodities: These include products like wheat, corn, soybeans, cotton, coffee, and livestock. Agricultural commodities are often influenced by factors such as weather conditions, crop yields, and supply and demand dynamics.

b. Energy Commodities: Energy commodities encompass crude oil, natural gas, heating oil, and gasoline. They play a crucial role in the global economy and are influenced by geopolitical events, production levels, and energy consumption patterns.

c. Metals: Metals are further divided into precious metals like gold, silver, platinum, and palladium, as well as industrial metals like copper, aluminum, and steel. Precious metals are often used for investment and hedging against economic uncertainties, while industrial metals are essential for manufacturing and construction.

d. Soft Commodities: Soft commodities include items like cocoa, sugar, coffee, and orange juice. They are derived from agricultural products and are often subject to price fluctuations based on weather conditions, disease outbreaks, and global supply chains.

e. Livestock and Meat: This category includes cattle, hogs, and various meat products. Livestock and meat commodities are influenced by factors such as livestock production, consumer preferences, and international trade.

Commodity trading involves buying and selling these raw materials in various forms, such as futures contracts, options, physical delivery, or through exchange-traded funds (ETFs). Commodity markets can be volatile, and the prices of commodities are influenced by a wide range of factors, including supply and demand dynamics, geopolitical events, weather conditions, and economic trends. Traders and investors participate in commodity markets to profit from price movements, hedge against risks, or diversify their investment portfolios.

The Role of Commodities in the Global Economy

Commodities play a fundamental role in the global economy due to their widespread use in production, consumption, and trade. Here are some key aspects of the role of commodities in the global economy:

1. **Resource Inputs**: Commodities serve as essential inputs for various industries. For instance, crude oil is a crucial input for the energy sector and petrochemical industry, while metals like copper are vital for construction and manufacturing. Without these commodities, many economic activities would be severely hindered or even impossible.

2. **Price Discovery**: Commodity markets help determine the prices of raw materials globally. These prices can have a significant impact on production costs and consumer prices. As such, commodities serve as a benchmark for pricing across industries.

3. **Inflation and Monetary Policy**: Changes in commodity prices, especially in energy and food, can influence inflation rates. Central banks and policymakers closely monitor commodity price movements when formulating monetary policies.

4. **Global Trade**: Commodities are among the most traded goods in international markets. Countries often specialize in the production of certain commodities and engage in global trade to access resources they lack domestically. This trade is critical for economic growth and development.

5. **Hedging and Risk Management**: Commodity markets offer tools like futures and options contracts that allow producers and consumers to hedge against price volatility. For example, a farmer can use futures contracts to lock in a price for their crops before harvesting, reducing the risk of price fluctuations.

6. **Investment and Diversification**: Commodities can serve as an investment asset class. Investors include commodities in their portfolios for diversification purposes and as a hedge against inflation or economic uncertainties. Precious metals like gold and silver are popular choices for this purpose.

7. **Geopolitical Impact**: The production and distribution of certain commodities can have geopolitical implications. Countries and regions with abundant resources may gain strategic importance in global politics, and conflicts can arise over access to these resources.

8. **Environmental Concerns**: The extraction and consumption of commodities can have significant environmental impacts. Issues such as deforestation, water usage, and carbon emissions are closely associated with the production of certain commodities, which has led to increased scrutiny and sustainability efforts.

9. **Food Security**: Agricultural commodities are crucial for food security. Changes in crop yields and food prices can affect the well-being of populations, making food commodities a critical component of global agricultural policies.

The Commodity Trading Ecosystem

The commodity trading ecosystem is a complex network of participants and institutions involved in the buying, selling, and trading of commodities. This ecosystem encompasses various stages of the commodity supply chain and includes a wide range of stakeholders. Here are the key components of the commodity trading ecosystem:

1. **Producers**: Producers are the entities responsible for extracting or growing commodities. They include farmers, miners, oil drillers, and ranchers. Producers are at the very beginning of the supply chain and are the source of the raw materials.

2. **Intermediaries and Aggregators**: Intermediaries, such as commodity brokers, traders, and cooperatives, often play a crucial role in aggregating and transporting commodities from producers to consumers. They may also provide storage facilities and financing to producers.

3. **Commodity Exchanges**: Commodity exchanges are organized marketplaces where standardized commodity contracts are traded. These exchanges provide a platform for buyers and sellers to transact in a transparent and regulated manner. Examples of commodity exchanges include the Chicago Mercantile Exchange (CME) for agricultural and financial products and the London Metal Exchange (LME) for metals.

4. **Consumers and End-Users**: These are businesses and industries that use commodities as inputs in their production processes. For example, manufacturers use metals like aluminum and copper, while the energy sector relies on crude oil and natural gas. Consumers of agricultural commodities include food processors and retailers.

5. **Speculators and Investors**: Speculators and investors participate in commodity markets with the goal of making a profit. They may not have a direct interest in the physical delivery of commodities but

use various financial instruments like futures contracts and options to speculate on price movements.

6. **Banks and Financial Institutions**: Banks and financial institutions provide financing and credit to various participants in the commodity trading ecosystem. They offer loans, trade finance, and hedging services to manage price risks.

7. **Regulators**: Regulatory authorities, such as the U.S. Commodity Futures Trading Commission (CFTC) and the European Securities and Markets Authority (ESMA), oversee and enforce rules and regulations governing commodity trading to ensure fair and transparent markets.

8. **Clearinghouses**: Clearinghouses act as intermediaries between buyers and sellers in the settlement of commodity contracts. They guarantee the fulfillment of contractual obligations, reducing counterparty risk. Clearinghouses also facilitate margin and collateral management.

9. **Market Analysts and Research Firms**: These entities provide market intelligence, research, and analysis to help participants make informed trading decisions. Their insights cover supply and demand dynamics, price trends, and geopolitical factors affecting commodities.

10. **Technology Providers**: Technology companies develop and maintain trading platforms, electronic trading systems, and data analytics tools that enable efficient and real-time trading and risk management in commodity markets.

11. **Government Agencies**: Government agencies in producing and consuming countries may play a role in regulating and supporting commodity markets. They can influence trade policies, subsidies, and import/export regulations that impact the commodity trading ecosystem.

12. **Environmental and Sustainability Organizations**: With increasing concerns about the environmental impact of commodity production, sustainability organizations and certifications have become important. They promote sustainable and responsible sourcing of commodities.

The commodity trading ecosystem is highly interconnected, and the activities of one participant can influence the entire supply chain and market dynamics. Understanding the roles and interactions of these various stakeholders is essential for anyone involved in commodity trading or investing in commodities. Additionally, the ecosystem is subject to evolving regulations and market trends, making it a dynamic and challenging environment to navigate.

Key Participants in Commodity Markets

Commodity markets involve a diverse range of participants, each with their own roles and objectives. These participants contribute to the functioning of commodity markets and can be categorized into several main groups:

1. **Producers**: Producers are the entities responsible for the extraction, cultivation, or production of commodities. They include:

◈ **Farmers**: Producers of agricultural commodities such as grains, livestock, and fruits.

◈ **Miners**: Producers of minerals and metals like gold, copper, and iron ore.

◈ **Oil Companies**: Producers of crude oil and natural gas.

◈ **Ranchers**: Producers of livestock and meat products.

◈ **Forestry Companies**: Producers of timber and wood products.

2. **Consumers and End-Users**: These participants are the ultimate consumers of commodities, using them as inputs in their production processes. They include:

◈ **Manufacturers**: Use metals, energy, and various raw materials in manufacturing processes.

◈ **Energy Companies**: Use crude oil, natural gas, and coal in power generation and fuel production.

◈ **Food Processors and Retailers**: Utilize agricultural commodities in food production and distribution.

◈ **Construction Companies**: Use metals and building materials in construction projects.

3. **Traders and Merchants**: These entities act as intermediaries, buying and selling commodities to profit from price differences or to meet supply and demand imbalances. They include:

◈ **Commodity Traders**: Engage in speculative trading, buying and selling commodities for profit.

◈ **Commodity Merchants**: Buy, store, and transport physical commodities, often providing financing to producers.

◈ **Commodity Brokers**: Facilitate trades on behalf of clients, connecting buyers and sellers.

4. **Commodity Exchanges**: These organized marketplaces provide a platform for standardized commodity contracts to be traded. Key exchanges include:

◈ **Chicago Mercantile Exchange (CME)**: Trades a wide range of agricultural and financial commodities.

◈ **Intercontinental Exchange (ICE)**: Specializes in energy, metals, and agricultural commodities.

◈ **London Metal Exchange (LME)**: Focuses on non-ferrous metals.

5. **Speculators and Investors**: These participants engage in commodity markets with the aim of making a profit. They include:

◈ **Hedge Funds**: Invest in commodities to diversify portfolios and seek returns.

◈ **Retail Investors**: Individual investors who trade commodities through brokerage accounts.

◈ **Institutional Investors**: Large organizations like pension funds that allocate capital to commodities.

6. **Banks and Financial Institutions**: Banks provide financing, credit, and derivative products to participants in commodity markets. They offer services such as trade finance, hedging, and risk management.

7. **Clearinghouses**: Clearinghouses act as intermediaries, ensuring the settlement of commodity contracts and reducing counterparty risk. They manage margin and collateral requirements.

8. **Regulatory Authorities**: Regulatory bodies, such as the U.S. Commodity Futures Trading Commission (CFTC) and the European Securities and Markets Authority (ESMA), oversee and enforce rules and regulations governing commodity trading to maintain market integrity.

9. **Market Analysts and Research Firms**: These entities provide market research, analysis, and insights to help participants make informed trading decisions. They track supply and demand factors, price trends, and geopolitical developments.

10. **Environmental and Sustainability Organizations**: With growing concerns about sustainability, these organizations promote responsible and sustainable practices in commodity production and trading. They often offer certifications and standards for environmentally friendly commodities.

11. **Government Agencies**: In producing and consuming countries, government agencies can influence commodity markets through trade policies, subsidies, and import/export regulations. They may also maintain strategic reserves of certain commodities.

12. **Technology Providers**: Technology companies develop and maintain trading platforms, electronic trading systems, and data analytics tools that enable efficient and real-time trading and risk management in commodity markets.

These participants collectively form a complex and interconnected ecosystem in commodity markets. The roles and actions of these stakeholders can impact price movements, supply chains, and the overall functioning of commodity markets, making it essential for anyone involved in commodity trading to understand their interactions and motivations. Additionally, regulatory changes and global events can influence the dynamics of commodity markets, adding further complexity to this ecosystem.

Chapter 2: Types of Commodities

Classification of Commodities

Commodities can be broadly classified into several categories based on their characteristics and usage. The main categories of commodities include:

a. **Agricultural Commodities**: These are products that originate from farming and include both food and non-food items. Agricultural commodities are subject to weather conditions, crop yields, and supply and demand dynamics. Some examples include:

⟐ **Grains**: Wheat, corn, rice, oats, and barley are staple grains used in various food products.

⟐ **Livestock**: Cattle, hogs, and poultry are raised for meat production.

⟐ **Softs**: These include commodities like cotton, sugar, coffee, cocoa, and orange juice.

⟐ **Oilseeds**: Soybeans, canola, and sunflower seeds are used to produce vegetable oils and meal for animal feed.

⟐ **Dairy**: Milk, cheese, and butter are common dairy products.

b. **Energy Commodities**: Energy commodities are essential for powering economies and include various forms of energy sources. They play a critical role in global energy production and consumption. Key energy commodities include:

⟐ **Crude Oil**: The primary source of petroleum products such as gasoline, diesel, and jet fuel.

◈ **Natural Gas**: Used for heating, electricity generation, and as a feedstock in various industries.

◈ **Coal**: Used in power plants and industrial processes, although its use is declining in some regions.

◈ **Electricity**: Traded in some markets as a commodity, with various sources of generation.

c. **Metals**: Metals are essential for construction, manufacturing, and various industrial applications. They can be further categorized into:

◈ **Precious Metals**: These include gold, silver, platinum, and palladium, which are often used for investment and jewelry.

◈ **Base Metals**: Copper, aluminum, zinc, lead, and nickel are commonly used in manufacturing and construction.

◈ **Industrial Metals**: This category includes metals used in specific industrial applications, such as tin, cobalt, and titanium.

d. **Soft Commodities**: Soft commodities primarily encompass agricultural products that are typically grown rather than mined or extracted. They are sensitive to factors like weather conditions and disease outbreaks. Examples include coffee, cocoa, sugar, cotton, and rubber.

e. **Exotic Commodities**: These are commodities that don't fit neatly into traditional categories but are still traded. Examples include carbon credits, rare earth metals, and emission allowances.

f. **Livestock and Meat**: This category includes live animals like cattle and hogs, as well as meat products such as beef, pork, and poultry.

g. **Fish and Seafood**: Fish and seafood products, both wild-caught and farmed, are traded commodities and include species like salmon, shrimp, and tuna.

h. **Forestry Products**: Timber, wood pulp, and paper products are part of this category, often used in construction and paper manufacturing.

i. **Renewable Energy**: As sustainability gains importance, commodities related to renewable energy sources, such as wind and solar power, are becoming increasingly relevant.

j. **Recyclables**: Some recyclable materials, like scrap metal and paper, are traded commodities due to their recycling and reuse in various industries.

These categories represent the diverse range of commodities that are bought and sold in global markets. Each category has its own supply and demand dynamics, price drivers, and factors influencing their trade. Understanding these classifications is essential for participants in commodity markets, as they impact trading strategies, risk management, and investment decisions.

Characteristics and Unique Features of Different Commodities

Commodities vary widely in their characteristics and unique features due to their diverse nature and uses in the global economy. Here's a closer look at some of these characteristics and features for different commodity categories:

Agricultural Commodities:

1. **Seasonality**: Many agricultural commodities are subject to seasonal production cycles and are heavily influenced by weather conditions. For example, planting and harvest seasons can significantly impact crop prices.

2. **Perishability**: Fresh agricultural products like fruits and vegetables are highly perishable, making storage and transportation logistics critical factors in their pricing and trade.

3. **Quality Grading**: Agricultural commodities often require grading based on quality parameters. Grading influences pricing, with higher-quality produce typically commanding higher prices.

4. **Government Subsidies**: Agricultural commodities are sometimes subject to government subsidies and support programs to stabilize prices and protect farmers.

Energy Commodities:

1. **Global Impact**: Energy commodities, particularly crude oil, have a profound impact on the global economy. Their prices can influence inflation rates, currency values, and geopolitical dynamics.

2. **Storage Challenges**: Crude oil and natural gas require specialized infrastructure for storage, transportation, and refining. Supply disruptions or excess supply can lead to price volatility.

3. **Environmental Concerns**: Energy commodities face increasing scrutiny due to environmental concerns, particularly in the context of climate change. Policies and regulations can affect their production and consumption.

Metals:

1. **Industrial and Precious Metals**: Precious metals like gold and silver are often used as stores of value and as safe-haven assets during times of economic uncertainty. Industrial metals like copper are closely tied to economic activity and construction.

2. **Cyclical Demand**: Metals are sensitive to economic cycles. During periods of economic growth, industrial metals tend to perform well, while precious metals may see reduced demand.

3. **Supply Concentration**: Some metals are produced by a limited number of countries or mining companies, leading to supply concentration risks.

Soft Commodities:

1. **Weather Volatility**: Soft commodities such as coffee, cocoa, and cotton are highly susceptible to weather conditions, including droughts, hurricanes, and diseases affecting crops.

2. **Supply Chain Complexity**: The production and processing of soft commodities often involve complex supply chains, with multiple intermediaries between producers and consumers.

Livestock and Meat:

1. **Feed Costs**: The cost of animal feed, which can be influenced by factors like grain prices, affects the profitability of livestock production.

2. **Health Concerns**: Outbreaks of diseases in livestock can have significant impacts on meat prices and trade, leading to supply disruptions.

Fish and Seafood:

1. **Sustainability**: Concerns about overfishing and the sustainability of fisheries have led to increased scrutiny and regulation in the seafood industry.

2. **Seasonal Variability**: The availability of certain fish species can be highly seasonal, affecting supply and pricing.

Renewable Energy:

1. **Technology Advances**: The renewable energy sector is characterized by rapid technological advancements, which can impact the competitiveness of different energy sources.

2. **Policy and Subsidies**: Government policies and subsidies often play a crucial role in the growth and adoption of renewable energy technologies.

Recyclables:

1. **Environmental Concerns**: Recycling commodities, like scrap metal and paper, are influenced by environmental concerns and regulations related to waste management and resource conservation.

2. **Global Trade**: Recyclable materials are traded globally, and market dynamics can be affected by international shipping and recycling facilities' capacities.

These characteristics and unique features make each commodity category distinct and subject to its own set of market forces and risks. Traders, investors, and businesses involved in commodity markets need to understand these nuances to make informed decisions and manage their exposure to commodity price fluctuations. Additionally, evolving global trends and regulatory changes can further impact the dynamics of commodity markets.

Global supply and demand dynamics play a central role in shaping commodity markets. Understanding these dynamics is essential for participants in commodity trading and investment. Here's an overview of how supply and demand factors influence commodity prices:

Supply Factors:

1. **Production Levels**: The quantity of a commodity produced by suppliers, whether it's agricultural, energy, or metals, is a critical factor. Changes in production levels can be influenced by factors like weather conditions, technological advancements, and government policies.

2. **Geopolitical Factors**: Political instability, conflicts, and trade disputes can disrupt the supply of commodities. For example, trade sanctions on a major oil-producing country can limit the global supply of crude oil.

3. **Technological Advances**: Innovations in extraction, cultivation, and production techniques can increase the supply of commodities. For example, advancements in shale oil drilling have significantly increased oil production in the United States.

4. **Supply Chain Disruptions**: Events such as natural disasters, labor strikes, or transportation disruptions can interrupt the supply chain and lead to temporary shortages, affecting prices.

5. **Regulations**: Government regulations, such as environmental restrictions on mining or quotas on agricultural production, can impact supply levels.

Demand Factors:

1. **Economic Growth**: Economic expansion typically leads to increased demand for commodities, particularly industrial metals and energy. Conversely, economic recessions can reduce demand.

2. **Population Growth**: As the global population grows, so does the overall demand for food, energy, and other essential commodities.

3. **Consumer Preferences**: Changing consumer preferences, such as a shift towards healthier diets or electric vehicles, can alter demand for specific commodities.

4. **Urbanization**: Urbanization trends lead to greater infrastructure development and increased consumption of construction materials like steel and cement.

5. **Technology and Innovation**: Advancements in technology can influence the demand for certain commodities. For example, the growth of electric vehicles drives up demand for metals like lithium and cobalt.

6. **Environmental Concerns**: Environmental awareness can lead to changes in consumption patterns. For instance, efforts to reduce carbon emissions may increase demand for renewable energy sources.

Price Mechanisms:

1. **Price Elasticity**: Different commodities have varying degrees of price elasticity of demand and supply. Inelastic commodities, such as gasoline, may see significant price fluctuations in response to small changes in supply or demand.

2. **Inventory Levels**: The amount of commodities held in storage can act as a buffer against supply shocks. Low inventory levels can make markets more vulnerable to price volatility.

3. **Speculation**: Speculators and investors in commodity markets can influence prices, especially in futures markets, where they bet on future price movements without the intention of taking physical delivery of the commodity.

4. **Currency Exchange Rates**: Commodity prices are often denominated in currencies, and fluctuations in exchange rates can impact the affordability and demand for commodities in different regions.

5. **Weather Events**: Weather patterns, such as droughts, floods, and hurricanes, can have a direct and immediate impact on the supply of agricultural commodities.

6. **Government Interventions**: Government policies, subsidies, and trade restrictions can distort supply and demand dynamics in commodity markets.

7. **Global Trade**: International trade in commodities allows regions to access resources they lack domestically. Trade agreements and tariffs can affect the flow of commodities across borders.

It's important to note that supply and demand dynamics can vary significantly among different commodities. For example, agricultural commodities are highly dependent on weather conditions and have relatively short planting-to-harvest cycles, while the development of new energy technologies can have a long-term impact on energy commodity demand.

Traders, investors, and businesses involved in commodity markets use a combination of fundamental analysis (assessing supply and demand fundamentals) and technical analysis (studying historical price patterns) to make informed decisions. They also monitor global events, policy changes, and market sentiment to anticipate and react to shifts in supply and demand dynamics that can influence commodity prices.

Seasonal patterns in commodity markets refer to recurring price trends and behavior that tend to happen at specific times of the year. These patterns are often driven by seasonal factors such as weather, agricultural cycles, and consumption patterns. Traders and investors closely monitor these patterns to make informed decisions. Here are some common examples of seasonal patterns in commodity markets:

Agricultural Commodities:

1. **Planting and Harvest Seasons**: Many agricultural commodities, such as grains (wheat, corn, soybeans), have distinct planting and harvesting seasons. Prices often show patterns of weakness leading up to harvest when supplies increase and strength leading into planting when uncertainty about crop conditions prevails.

2. **Weather-Dependent Variability**: Weather events like droughts, floods, and hurricanes can significantly impact crop yields and prices. For example, a dry summer can lead to a surge in grain prices due to lower crop production.

3. **Livestock**: The livestock sector also experiences seasonal patterns. For instance, cattle prices tend to rise in the spring as ranchers bring animals to market, while poultry prices may see fluctuations related to holiday demand.

Energy Commodities:

1. **Winter and Summer Demand**: Energy commodities like natural gas and heating oil often exhibit seasonal patterns based on weather-related demand. Prices tend to rise in the winter as households and businesses increase heating needs. Conversely, prices may dip in the summer when demand for heating decreases.

2. **Hurricane Season**: In the oil markets, the hurricane season in the Gulf of Mexico can disrupt oil production and cause price spikes during the summer and fall months.

Metals:

1. **Construction Season**: Industrial metals like copper and steel are influenced by construction activity. Prices may rise in the spring and summer when construction projects are in full swing.

2. **Precious Metals**: Precious metals like gold often exhibit seasonal patterns related to jewelry demand and festivals in various cultures. For example, gold demand tends to increase in the run-up to the Indian wedding season.

Soft Commodities:

1. **Coffee and Cocoa**: Coffee and cocoa prices can be influenced by weather patterns in major producing regions. Dry weather can lead to lower yields and higher prices.

2. **Sugar**: Sugar prices can show seasonal patterns based on harvest cycles, with prices often declining during the harvest season and rising during the off-season.

Financial Commodities:

1. **Interest Rates**: While not physical commodities, interest rate futures exhibit seasonal patterns related to central bank policies and economic cycles. For instance, interest rate futures may show patterns of strength in anticipation of rate hikes by central banks.

2. **Precious Metals**: Gold and silver may have seasonally stronger periods related to geopolitical events, economic uncertainty, and currency fluctuations.

It's important to note that while seasonal patterns can be reliable, they are not guaranteed to repeat every year. Factors such as changing weather patterns, evolving consumer behavior, and unexpected events (e.g., natural disasters) can disrupt historical patterns. Additionally, financial market participants often incorporate seasonal considerations into their trading strategies, which can lead to adjustments in market behavior.

Traders and investors should use seasonal patterns as one of several tools in their analysis and decision-making processes, alongside fundamental analysis, technical analysis, and a thorough understanding of current market conditions and global events.

Chapter 3: Commodity Trading Strategies

Speculation vs. Hedging in Commodity Trading

Commodity trading can be broadly categorized into two primary approaches: speculation and hedging. These strategies serve different purposes and cater to the needs of different market participants.

Speculation:

1. **Objective**: Speculation involves buying or selling commodities with the primary goal of profiting from anticipated price movements. Speculators are not directly involved in the production, consumption, or physical delivery of the underlying commodities; they seek to profit from price changes in the futures or spot markets.

2. **Risk Profile**: Speculators accept a higher level of risk because they are exposed to price fluctuations in the market. Their positions can result in gains or losses based on price movements.

3. **Participants**: Speculators include individual traders, hedge funds, proprietary trading firms, and other market participants looking to capitalize on price volatility. They are not typically involved in the physical production or consumption of the commodity.

4. **Trading Instruments**: Speculators often use futures contracts, options, exchange-traded funds (ETFs), or other derivative products to take positions in commodities. These instruments allow them to profit from both rising and falling prices.

5. **Time Horizon**: Speculators may have short-term or long-term investment horizons, depending on their trading strategies. Some

engage in day trading, while others adopt a longer-term investment approach.

6. **Examples**: A speculator might buy crude oil futures with the expectation that geopolitical tensions will lead to higher oil prices or sell wheat futures in anticipation of a bumper crop that will depress prices.

Hedging:

1. **Objective**: Hedging involves using commodity derivatives to mitigate or offset the risks associated with price fluctuations in the underlying commodity. Hedgers are typically producers, consumers, or businesses with exposure to commodity price movements. Their primary goal is to protect against adverse price changes.

2. **Risk Profile**: Hedgers seek to reduce risk and price volatility. They are willing to incur some costs (such as option premiums) to protect against unfavorable price movements.

3. **Participants**: Hedgers can include farmers, mining companies, energy producers, airlines, manufacturers, and other businesses with exposure to commodity prices. They use hedging to stabilize their revenue or cost structures.

4. **Trading Instruments**: Hedgers use futures contracts, options, swaps, and other derivative instruments to manage price risk. By taking positions opposite to their physical commodity exposure, they can offset potential losses.

5. **Time Horizon**: Hedging positions are typically held for the duration of the risk exposure. For example, a farmer may hedge the price of their crops from planting to harvest.

6. **Examples**: An airline may hedge against rising jet fuel prices by purchasing fuel futures to lock in a set price for future deliveries. A farmer might hedge against falling grain prices by selling futures contracts to guarantee a minimum selling price.

In summary, speculation and hedging represent two distinct approaches to commodity trading, each serving a different purpose:

◈ **Speculation** involves trading commodities with the aim of profiting from price movements. It is driven by market analysis and a view on future price direction.

◈ **Hedging** involves using commodity derivatives to manage and reduce price risk. It is a risk management strategy aimed at protecting against adverse price fluctuations.

Both approaches are essential to the functioning of commodity markets. Speculators provide liquidity and help discover prices, while hedgers use the market to manage their exposure to price volatility, ensuring the stability of their operations and finances.

In commodity trading, participants often use various trading approaches to make informed decisions about when to buy or sell commodities. Two fundamental approaches widely employed are technical analysis and fundamental analysis. Here's an overview of each approach:

1. Technical Analysis:

Technical analysis involves studying historical price and volume data of commodities, as well as chart patterns and technical indicators, to predict future price movements. It assumes that historical price patterns and trends tend to repeat themselves and that market sentiment is reflected in price charts. Key aspects of technical analysis include:

◈ **Price Charts**: Traders use various types of price charts, such as candlestick charts or bar charts, to visualize historical price data.

◈ **Trends**: Technical analysts identify trends, including uptrends (rising prices), downtrends (falling prices), and sideways trends (range-bound prices).

◈ **Support and Resistance Levels**: Traders look for levels at which prices tend to find support (stop falling) or encounter resistance (stop rising). These levels are often used for setting entry and exit points.

◈ **Technical Indicators**: Various indicators, like moving averages, Relative Strength Index (RSI), and Moving Average Convergence Divergence (MACD), help traders identify potential trend changes, overbought or oversold conditions, and momentum.

◈ **Pattern Recognition**: Chart patterns such as head and shoulders, double tops/bottoms, flags, and triangles are used to anticipate future price movements based on historical patterns.

2. Fundamental Analysis:

Fundamental analysis focuses on examining the underlying factors that affect commodity prices. It involves studying the supply and demand fundamentals of the commodity, as well as broader economic, geopolitical, and environmental factors. Key aspects of fundamental analysis include:

◈ **Supply and Demand**: Analysts assess factors like production levels, consumption patterns, and inventories to gauge the balance between supply and demand. For example, a forecast of a bumper crop might indicate a potential oversupply of agricultural commodities.

◈ **Weather and Climate**: Weather conditions can have a significant impact on agricultural commodities. Droughts, floods, and extreme weather events can affect crop yields.

◈ **Geopolitical Events**: Events such as trade disputes, conflicts in major producing regions, and political instability can disrupt supply chains and influence prices.

◈ **Economic Indicators**: Economic data like GDP growth, employment figures, and consumer spending can provide insights into demand for commodities. Strong economic growth may lead to increased consumption of energy and metals.

◈ **Currency Movements**: Commodity prices are often quoted in currency denominations. Changes in currency exchange rates can affect the affordability and demand for commodities in different regions.

◈ **Government Policies and Regulations**: Government actions, subsidies, trade policies, and environmental regulations can impact commodity markets. For instance, a government ban on commodity exports can affect global supply.

Choosing Between Technical and Fundamental Analysis:

◈ **Trading Style**: Traders often choose between technical and fundamental analysis based on their trading style. Short-term traders may favor technical analysis for its focus on price patterns and intraday movements, while long-term investors may rely more on fundamental analysis to assess a commodity's intrinsic value.

◈ **Commodity Type**: The choice of analysis may also depend on the type of commodity being traded. Agricultural commodities are often influenced by fundamental factors like crop reports and weather, while metals and energy commodities may respond to both technical and fundamental factors.

⟐ **Risk Tolerance**: Traders with a lower risk tolerance may prefer fundamental analysis, which provides a broader understanding of market dynamics and can help mitigate risks associated with sudden price movements.

⟐ **Combination**: Some traders use a combination of both technical and fundamental analysis to gain a comprehensive view of the market. This approach allows them to consider both short-term price trends and longer-term supply and demand dynamics.

Ultimately, the choice between technical and fundamental analysis—or a combination of both—depends on the trader's preferences, objectives, and the specific commodity being traded. Successful traders often develop their own strategies based on these approaches and adapt them to changing market conditions.

1. Futures Contracts:

⟐ **Definition**: Futures contracts are standardized agreements between two parties to buy or sell a specific quantity of a commodity at a predetermined price on a specified future date. These contracts are traded on organized exchanges.

⟐ **Purpose**: Futures contracts are commonly used for both speculation and hedging. Speculators aim to profit from price movements, while hedgers use futures to manage and mitigate price risk.

⟐ **Characteristics**:

⟐ Standardized: Futures contracts have standardized terms, including contract size, delivery date, and quality specifications.

⟐ Margin Requirements: Traders must post an initial margin and potentially maintain a maintenance margin to cover potential losses.

◈ Physical or Cash Settlement: Some futures contracts require physical delivery of the commodity, while others settle in cash based on the contract's final price.

◈ **Example**: An oil producer might sell crude oil futures contracts to lock in a price for their future production. Alternatively, a trader might buy gold futures contracts with the expectation that gold prices will rise.

2. Options Contracts:

◈ **Definition**: Options contracts give the holder the right (but not the obligation) to buy (call option) or sell (put option) a commodity at a predetermined price (strike price) before or on a specified future date. Options can be traded on organized exchanges or in over-the-counter (OTC) markets.

◈ **Purpose**: Options are used for various purposes, including speculation, hedging, and risk management. They provide flexibility to traders.

◈ **Characteristics**:

◈ Premium: The buyer of an option pays a premium to the seller for the right to exercise the option.

◈ Limited Risk: Option buyers have limited risk to the premium paid, while sellers have potentially unlimited risk.

◈ American vs. European Style: American options can be exercised at any time before expiration, while European options can only be exercised at expiration.

◈ **Example**: A farmer may buy put options on their crop to protect against falling prices. A speculator might buy call options on natural gas if they anticipate a price increase.

3. Swaps:

◈ **Definition**: Swaps are customized agreements between two parties to exchange cash flows based on the price movements of commodities. Unlike futures and options, swaps are typically traded over the counter (OTC) and are not standardized.

◈ **Purpose**: Swaps are commonly used for hedging and managing specific price risks. They provide flexibility to tailor the terms of the agreement to the parties' needs.

◈ **Characteristics**:

◈ Customization: Swaps can be customized to match the exact requirements of the parties involved, including the commodities involved, notional amounts, and pricing formulas.

◈ Counterparty Risk: Swaps expose participants to counterparty risk, as they are bilateral agreements. Counterparty risk can be managed through credit arrangements.

◈ **Types**:

◈ **Commodity Price Swaps**: These involve the exchange of cash flows based on the price movement of a specific commodity.

◈ **Interest Rate Swaps**: While not directly tied to commodities, interest rate swaps are relevant for commodity producers and consumers managing financing costs.

◈ **Example**: An energy producer might enter into a commodity price swap to receive a fixed price for their oil production in exchange for paying a floating market price.

Traders, hedgers, and investors choose from these instruments based on their risk tolerance, objectives, and market conditions. The choice between futures, options, and swaps depends on factors like the desired level of customization, cost considerations, and the need for physical delivery or cash settlement. Additionally, participants often use a combination of these instruments to build comprehensive trading and risk management strategies.

Different commodity trading strategies come with varying risk-reward profiles, reflecting the trade-off between the potential for profit and the exposure to potential losses. Traders and investors should carefully assess these profiles to align their strategies with their risk tolerance, financial goals, and market expectations. Here's an overview of the risk-reward profiles of some common commodity trading strategies:

1. Speculation:

◈ **Risk Profile**: Speculation is generally associated with higher levels of risk. Speculators aim to profit from price movements, but they can incur significant losses if market conditions move against their positions.

◈ **Reward Profile**: The potential for profit in speculation is relatively high, as speculators can profit from both rising and falling prices. However, the degree of profit or loss depends on the extent of price movement and the size of the position.

◈ **Risk Management**: Speculators often use stop-loss orders to limit potential losses and employ position sizing strategies to manage risk.

2. Hedging:

◈ **Risk Profile**: Hedging is primarily a risk management strategy. It aims to reduce or eliminate the risk of adverse price movements in the underlying commodity. While hedging mitigates risk, it may involve costs such as option premiums or reduced potential profits if prices move favorably.

◈ **Reward Profile**: The primary goal of hedging is not profit maximization but risk reduction. As such, the potential for substantial profits is limited. However, it allows businesses to stabilize revenue or costs.

◈ **Risk Management**: Hedgers often accept the trade-off of limited profit potential in exchange for reduced exposure to adverse price movements.

3. Spread Trading:

◈ **Risk Profile**: Spread trading involves taking opposing positions in related contracts or commodities to profit from the price difference between them. It typically has a lower risk profile compared to outright speculation, as it hedges against certain price movements.

◈ **Reward Profile**: The potential for profit in spread trading is typically lower compared to pure speculation. Spread traders aim to capture small price differentials between related contracts, leading to more modest returns.

◈ **Risk Management**: Spread trading strategies aim to reduce directional risk by simultaneously holding long and short positions, mitigating the impact of market-wide price movements.

4. Trend Following:

◈ **Risk Profile**: Trend-following strategies involve trading in the direction of prevailing market trends. They can experience periods of drawdowns and losses when markets move against the trend.

◈ **Reward Profile**: Trend-following strategies aim to capture profits during sustained price trends. The potential for significant gains exists during strong, persistent trends.

◈ **Risk Management**: Risk management in trend-following strategies typically involves setting stop-loss orders to limit losses during trend reversals.

5. Arbitrage:

◈ **Risk Profile**: Arbitrage seeks to profit from price discrepancies between related assets or markets. It generally has a lower risk profile because it involves simultaneous buying and selling to capture price differences.

◈ **Reward Profile**: Arbitrage opportunities often offer low-risk, low-reward scenarios. Profits are typically small per trade, but they can accumulate over time with high-frequency trading.

◈ **Risk Management**: Arbitrageurs aim to minimize execution risk and monitor markets closely to seize fleeting price disparities.

6. Carry Trade:

◈ **Risk Profile**: Carry trading involves borrowing in a currency with a low-interest rate and investing in a currency with a higher interest rate. It carries foreign exchange rate risk and potential interest rate changes.

◈ **Reward Profile**: Carry trades aim to generate returns from the interest rate differential between currencies. The potential for profit depends on the interest rate spread and exchange rate movements.

◈ **Risk Management**: Carry traders may use stop-loss orders to limit losses from adverse exchange rate movements and closely monitor interest rate differentials.

It's important to note that individual strategies within each category can vary in risk-reward profiles. Additionally, market conditions, volatility, and the specific implementation of a strategy can impact the potential for profit and loss. Traders and investors should thoroughly understand their chosen strategy, have a clear risk management plan in place, and be prepared for the possibility of losses in commodity trading. Diversifying across different strategies or asset classes can also help manage overall risk.

Chapter 4: Commodity Market Fundamentals

Understanding Supply and Demand in Commodity Markets

Supply and demand are the foundational principles that drive commodity markets. An understanding of these fundamentals is crucial for participants in commodity trading and investment. Here's a comprehensive look at supply and demand dynamics in commodity markets:

Supply Factors:

1. **Production Levels**: The quantity of a commodity produced by suppliers is a fundamental driver of supply. Production levels can be influenced by factors such as weather conditions, technological advancements, and government policies.

2. **Weather and Climate**: Weather events, including droughts, floods, hurricanes, and extreme temperatures, can significantly impact the supply of agricultural commodities and energy resources.

3. **Geopolitical Factors**: Political instability, conflicts, trade disputes, and government regulations in major producing regions can disrupt supply chains and affect commodity availability.

4. **Technological Advances**: Innovations in extraction, cultivation, and production techniques can increase the supply of commodities. For example, new drilling technologies have boosted oil and natural gas production.

5. **Transportation and Infrastructure**: The availability and efficiency of transportation and distribution networks play a role in determining

the supply of commodities. Infrastructure improvements can lead to increased supply.

6. **Environmental Factors**: Environmental regulations, conservation efforts, and sustainability initiatives can impact the production and supply of commodities. For instance, restrictions on logging can affect the supply of timber.

Demand Factors:

1. **Economic Growth**: Economic expansion typically leads to increased demand for commodities, particularly industrial metals and energy resources. Conversely, economic recessions can reduce demand.

2. **Population Growth**: As the global population grows, the overall demand for food, energy, and other essential commodities also increases.

3. **Consumer Preferences**: Changing consumer preferences, such as a shift toward healthier diets or electric vehicles, can alter demand for specific commodities.

4. **Urbanization**: Urbanization trends lead to greater infrastructure development and increased consumption of construction materials like steel and cement.

5. **Technology and Innovation**: Advancements in technology can influence the demand for certain commodities. For example, the growth of electric vehicles drives up demand for metals like lithium and cobalt.

6. **Environmental Concerns**: Environmental awareness can lead to changes in consumption patterns. Efforts to reduce carbon emissions may increase demand for renewable energy sources.

Price Mechanisms:

1. **Price Elasticity**: Different commodities have varying degrees of price elasticity of demand and supply. Inelastic commodities, such as gasoline, may see significant price fluctuations in response to small changes in supply or demand.

2. **Inventory Levels**: The amount of commodities held in storage can act as a buffer against supply shocks. Low inventory levels can make markets more vulnerable to price volatility.

3. **Speculation**: Speculators and investors in commodity markets can influence prices, especially in futures markets, where they bet on future price movements without the intention of taking physical delivery of the commodity.

4. **Currency Exchange Rates**: Commodity prices are often denominated in currencies, and fluctuations in exchange rates can impact the affordability and demand for commodities in different regions.

5. **Weather Events**: Weather patterns, such as droughts, floods, and hurricanes, can have a direct and immediate impact on the supply of agricultural commodities.

6. **Government Interventions**: Government policies, subsidies, and trade restrictions can distort supply and demand dynamics in commodity markets.

7. **Global Trade**: International trade in commodities allows regions to access resources they lack domestically. Trade agreements and tariffs can affect the flow of commodities across borders.

Understanding the interplay between supply and demand factors is essential for participants in commodity markets. Traders, investors, and businesses use this knowledge to make informed decisions about when to buy or sell commodities and to manage their exposure to commodity price fluctuations. Additionally, staying informed about evolving global trends and regulatory changes is critical, as these factors can further impact the dynamics of commodity markets.

Market Influences: Weather, Geopolitical Events, and Regulations

Commodity markets are highly sensitive to a range of external factors and influences that can impact supply, demand, and prices. Three significant market influences in commodity markets are weather, geopolitical events, and regulations:

1. Weather:

◈ **Impact on Agriculture**: Weather conditions play a critical role in agricultural commodity markets. Factors like rainfall, temperature, and the occurrence of extreme weather events (droughts, floods, hurricanes) directly affect crop yields. For example, a prolonged drought can lead to lower wheat or corn production, causing prices to rise.

◈ **Energy Commodities**: Weather events can disrupt the production and distribution of energy commodities. Hurricanes in the Gulf of Mexico, for instance, can lead to the evacuation of offshore oil platforms and refineries, reducing oil and gas supply and driving up prices.

◈ **Renewable Energy**: Weather patterns also influence renewable energy production. Solar and wind energy generation is dependent on weather conditions, impacting electricity supply and pricing in regions with high renewable energy penetration.

2. Geopolitical Events:

◈ **Supply Disruptions**: Geopolitical events such as conflicts, trade disputes, and sanctions can disrupt the supply of commodities. For example, trade tensions between major economies can lead to tariffs on commodities like steel and aluminum, affecting global supply chains.

◈ **Energy Security**: Political instability in major oil-producing regions, such as the Middle East, can create uncertainty in energy markets. Geopolitical tensions can lead to supply disruptions, causing oil prices to spike.

◈ **Commodity Export Bans**: Some countries may impose export bans or restrictions on key commodities to ensure domestic supply, affecting global commodity markets. For instance, a country might ban the export of rice during a shortage.

3. Regulations:

◈ **Environmental Regulations**: Environmental regulations can have a significant impact on commodity markets. For example, stricter emissions standards may lead to increased demand for cleaner-burning fuels, affecting the energy sector.

◈ **Trade Policies**: Government trade policies, including tariffs and import/export restrictions, can influence the flow of commodities across borders. Trade agreements and trade disputes can affect the competitiveness of certain commodities.

◈ **Commodity-Specific Regulations**: Commodity markets are subject to specific regulations. For instance, agricultural commodity markets often have regulations governing crop planting, quality standards, and subsidies.

◈ **Financial Regulations**: Financial regulations can impact commodity markets, particularly in the case of commodity derivatives trading. Regulatory changes may affect the participation of financial institutions and speculators in commodity futures and options markets.

It's important to note that these influences are interconnected. For example, a geopolitical event in a major oil-producing region can impact energy markets, and regulatory changes aimed at reducing carbon emissions can influence the demand for specific energy commodities.

Participants in commodity markets, whether they are producers, consumers, speculators, or investors, need to stay informed about these external factors and their potential impacts. Strategies and risk management plans should take into account the possibility of supply disruptions, price volatility, and regulatory changes. Additionally, market participants often use these influences as part of their fundamental analysis to make informed trading and investment decisions in commodity markets.

Here are some key market reports and data sources commonly used by participants in commodity trading:

Market Reports:

1. **USDA Crop Reports**: The United States Department of Agriculture (USDA) releases regular reports on crop production, planting intentions, and crop conditions. These reports are crucial for agricultural commodity traders and provide insights into the supply and demand dynamics of crops like corn, wheat, and soybeans.

2. **EIA Energy Reports**: The U.S. Energy Information Administration (EIA) publishes reports on energy production, consumption, and inventories. These reports cover crude oil, natural gas, and other energy commodities, helping traders assess supply and demand trends.

3. **IEA Oil Market Reports**: The International Energy Agency (IEA) releases monthly oil market reports that provide data on global oil supply, demand, and inventory levels. These reports are closely monitored by oil traders and investors.

4. **OPEC Monthly Oil Market Report**: The Organization of the Petroleum Exporting Countries (OPEC) publishes monthly reports on the oil market, including production levels, forecasts, and analysis of global supply and demand trends.

5. **Metals Market Reports**: Various organizations and exchanges provide market reports for metals like gold, silver, copper, and aluminum. These reports include data on production, consumption, and inventory levels.

6. **Weather Reports**: Weather data services and agencies provide forecasts and reports on weather conditions, which are crucial for assessing the impact on agricultural commodities. Traders closely monitor weather reports for crop-growing regions to anticipate potential supply disruptions.

Data Sources:

1. **Commodity Exchanges**: Commodity futures exchanges like the Chicago Mercantile Exchange (CME Group), Intercontinental Exchange (ICE), and others provide real-time data on commodity futures prices, trading volumes, and open interest.

2. **Government Agencies**: Government agencies, such as the USDA, EIA, and Bureau of Labor Statistics (BLS), offer valuable data on agricultural production, energy consumption, and economic indicators that impact commodity markets.

3. **Financial News Services**: Financial news outlets like Bloomberg, Reuters, and CNBC offer comprehensive coverage of commodity markets, including real-time prices, market analysis, and expert commentary.

4. **Commodity Price Websites**: Numerous websites and online platforms provide free and subscription-based access to commodity

price data, historical charts, and market analysis. Examples include Investing.com, MarketWatch, and TradingView.

5. **Commodity Research Firms**: Research firms specializing in commodities, such as S&P Global Platts and IHS Markit, provide in-depth market analysis, forecasts, and research reports for various commodity sectors.

6. **Commodity Trading Software**: Trading platforms and software often come with built-in data feeds and analytics tools for traders to access real-time market data, technical indicators, and charting capabilities.

7. **Industry Associations**: Industry-specific associations and organizations may publish reports and data relevant to their respective commodity sectors. For example, the American Petroleum Institute (API) releases weekly data on U.S. crude oil inventories.

8. **Government Commodity Boards**: In some countries, government commodity boards or marketing boards provide information on commodity production, prices, and market conditions.

Traders and investors in commodity markets often use a combination of these reports and data sources to conduct fundamental analysis, assess market trends, and make trading decisions. Staying informed and having access to reliable and up-to-date information is essential for effectively navigating the dynamic and often volatile world of commodity trading.

Commodity exchanges play a crucial role in the functioning of commodity markets by providing a centralized platform for the trading and price discovery of various commodities. These exchanges serve as essential intermediaries that facilitate transactions between market participants, including producers, consumers, traders, and investors. Here are the key roles and functions of commodity exchanges:

1. **Price Discovery**: Commodity exchanges provide a transparent and efficient mechanism for determining market prices. Prices are determined through the interaction of buyers and sellers in the exchange's trading pits or electronic trading platforms. These publicly available prices serve as reference points for commodities, helping market participants make informed decisions.

2. **Risk Management**: Commodity exchanges offer a range of derivative products, such as futures and options contracts, that allow market participants to manage and mitigate price risk. Hedgers use these instruments to lock in prices for future transactions, reducing exposure to price volatility. Speculators use derivatives for investment and profit-seeking purposes.

3. **Market Liquidity**: Exchanges enhance market liquidity by bringing together a wide range of market participants. The presence of numerous buyers and sellers on the exchange allows for easier entry and exit from positions. This liquidity contributes to lower bid-ask spreads and reduces the cost of trading.

4. **Standardization**: Commodity exchanges standardize the terms of futures and options contracts, including contract size, quality specifications, delivery methods, and expiration dates. Standardization ensures that all market participants are trading under the same terms, promoting fairness and efficiency.

5. **Clearing and Settlement**: Exchanges typically have a clearinghouse that acts as a counterparty to all trades. This central clearing function ensures the performance of contracts, including the transfer of ownership and payment. It reduces counterparty risk and ensures the integrity of the market.

6. **Storage and Delivery Facilities**: Some commodity exchanges provide or oversee storage and delivery facilities for physical

commodities. These facilities are essential for commodities that are delivered upon the expiration of futures contracts. Exchanges ensure the quality and availability of storage and delivery infrastructure.

7. **Regulation and Oversight**: Commodity exchanges are subject to regulatory oversight to maintain market integrity and protect the interests of market participants. Regulatory authorities set rules and monitor exchange operations to prevent fraud, manipulation, and unfair practices.

8. **Information Dissemination**: Exchanges often disseminate market data, including real-time prices, trading volumes, and open interest, to market participants and the public. This information is valuable for traders, investors, and analysts for making informed decisions.

9. **Education and Training**: Exchanges may offer educational programs and training for market participants, helping them better understand commodity markets, trading strategies, and risk management techniques.

10. **Market Development**: Exchanges actively work to develop and expand commodity markets. They introduce new contracts, explore innovative products, and seek to attract a diverse range of market participants, including institutional investors.

11. **Market Integrity**: Exchanges enforce rules and regulations that promote market integrity. This includes monitoring for market manipulation, fraud, and excessive speculation to maintain a fair and orderly marketplace.

12. **Global Connectivity**: Many commodity exchanges are interconnected with global markets, allowing for cross-border trading and hedging. This connectivity facilitates international trade and risk management.

Overall, commodity exchanges are pivotal in ensuring the efficient and transparent operation of commodity markets. They provide the infrastructure, rules, and services necessary for market participants to buy, sell, and manage the risks associated with commodities, contributing to price stability and the functioning of global commodity supply chains.

Chapter 5: Risk Management in Commodity Trading

Types of Risks in Commodity Trading (Price, Credit, Operational, Counterparty)

Commodity trading involves a variety of risks that participants must manage to protect their investments and achieve their financial goals. These risks can broadly be categorized into several key types:

1. Price Risk:

Price risk, also known as market risk, is one of the most significant risks in commodity trading. It arises from the volatility and uncertainty of commodity prices. Price risk can affect both buyers and sellers and can result in financial losses if commodity prices move unfavorably. Key aspects of price risk include:

◈ **Price Volatility**: Commodities often experience price fluctuations due to factors like supply and demand imbalances, geopolitical events, weather conditions, and economic developments.

◈ **Long and Short Positions**: Buyers face the risk of prices rising (adverse price movements), while sellers face the risk of prices falling (adverse price movements). Participants need to manage these directional risks.

◈ **Hedging**: One way to mitigate price risk is through hedging using derivative instruments like futures and options contracts. Hedging allows market participants to lock in prices and protect against adverse price movements.

2. Credit Risk:

Credit risk, also known as counterparty risk, arises from the possibility that one party in a transaction may fail to meet its financial obligations. In commodity trading, credit risk can be significant, especially in over-the-counter (OTC) transactions. Key aspects of credit risk include:

◈ **Counterparty Default**: If a counterparty defaults on a trade, the non-defaulting party may suffer financial losses, including the loss of the commodity or the funds involved in the transaction.

◈ **Credit Assessment**: Market participants often conduct credit assessments and due diligence on their counterparties to assess their creditworthiness and minimize credit risk.

◈ **Clearinghouses**: The use of central clearinghouses in exchange-traded commodity contracts can reduce counterparty risk by acting as an intermediary that guarantees the performance of trades.

3. Operational Risk:

Operational risk refers to the risk of financial losses or disruptions resulting from internal processes, systems, human error, or external events. In commodity trading, operational risk can impact various aspects of trading and settlement processes. Key aspects of operational risk include:

◈ **Trade Execution Errors**: Mistakes in trade execution, such as incorrect order placement or miscommunication, can lead to financial losses.

◈ **Technology Failures**: System failures, outages, or cybersecurity breaches can disrupt trading activities and lead to operational losses.

◈ **Settlement and Delivery Issues**: Errors or delays in settlement and delivery processes can result in financial losses or contractual disputes.

4. Counterparty Risk:

Counterparty risk is a subset of credit risk and specifically relates to the creditworthiness of the party with whom a trade is executed. It is the risk that the counterparty may not fulfill its contractual obligations. Counterparty risk can be managed through credit assessments, collateral agreements, and the use of clearinghouses.

5. Regulatory and Compliance Risk:

Regulatory and compliance risks arise from the potential for changes in laws, regulations, or government policies that can impact commodity trading activities. Failure to comply with applicable regulations can result in legal and financial consequences.

6. Liquidity Risk:

Liquidity risk is the risk of not being able to buy or sell a commodity quickly without causing significant price fluctuations. Illiquid markets can lead to larger spreads, increased trading costs, and challenges in executing large orders.

7. Political and Geopolitical Risk:

Political and geopolitical risks stem from government actions, trade disputes, conflicts, or events in major producing regions. These risks can disrupt supply chains and affect commodity prices and availability.

8. Environmental Risk:

Environmental risks relate to the potential impact of environmental factors, such as climate change or environmental regulations, on commodity production, transportation, and demand. These risks can affect commodity prices and supply.

Effectively managing these various types of risks is essential for participants in commodity trading. Risk management strategies may involve the use of derivatives for hedging, credit assessments and collateral agreements, diversification, monitoring of regulatory changes, and robust operational processes. Risk management practices should be tailored to the specific needs and objectives of market participants and may evolve over time as market conditions change.

Risk identification and assessment are critical steps in the risk management process for commodity trading. By systematically identifying and assessing risks, traders, investors, and businesses can develop strategies to mitigate or manage these risks effectively. Here's how risk identification and assessment are typically conducted in commodity trading:

1. Risk Identification:

a. Price Risk:

� Identify the commodities or positions exposed to price volatility.

� Consider factors like historical price movements, market fundamentals, and external influences on commodity prices.

� Recognize whether the position is long (exposed to rising prices) or short (exposed to falling prices).

b. Credit Risk:

� Identify counterparties in trading transactions, especially in OTC trades.

� Assess the creditworthiness of counterparties by considering their financial stability, credit history, and industry reputation.

◈ Recognize potential exposure to counterparty default and quantify it.

c. Operational Risk:

◈ Identify potential operational weaknesses or vulnerabilities in trading processes.

◈ Consider factors such as trade execution errors, technology failures, and settlement and delivery processes.

◈ Recognize the impact of operational disruptions on trading activities.

d. Regulatory and Compliance Risk:

◈ Stay informed about relevant regulations and compliance requirements that apply to commodity trading.

◈ Identify areas where non-compliance could occur and assess the associated risks.

◈ Recognize the potential legal and financial consequences of regulatory violations.

e. Liquidity Risk:

◈ Identify commodities or positions that may be illiquid or have limited trading activity.

◈ Consider the potential impact of illiquidity on the ability to buy or sell at desired prices.

◈ Recognize the need for contingency plans in illiquid markets.

f. Political and Geopolitical Risk:

◈ Identify commodities or regions that may be susceptible to political or geopolitical events.

◈ Consider factors such as government policies, trade disputes, conflicts, and stability in major producing regions.

◈ Recognize how political and geopolitical events can disrupt supply chains and affect commodity markets.

g. Environmental Risk:

◈ Identify commodities or industries that may be exposed to environmental risks.

◈ Consider factors like climate change, environmental regulations, and sustainability initiatives.

◈ Recognize how environmental factors can impact commodity production, transportation, and demand.

2. Risk Assessment:

Once risks are identified, they should be assessed to determine their potential impact and likelihood. This assessment helps prioritize risks and allocate resources for risk management strategies. Common steps in risk assessment include:

a. Quantitative Assessment:

◈ Use historical data, statistical models, and market analysis to quantify the potential financial impact of price risk.

◈ Assess credit risk by estimating potential losses in the event of counterparty default.

◈ Consider the potential financial impact of operational failures or regulatory violations.

b. Qualitative Assessment:

◈ Evaluate qualitative factors that may not be easily quantifiable, such as reputational risk or the impact of political events.

◈ Consider the likelihood of regulatory changes and their impact on compliance risk.

◈ Assess the operational impact of technology failures or errors.

c. Scenario Analysis:

◈ Conduct scenario analysis to assess how different risk scenarios could affect trading positions or portfolios.

◈ Consider worst-case scenarios and stress tests to evaluate the resilience of risk management strategies.

d. Risk Prioritization:

◈ Prioritize risks based on their potential impact and likelihood.

◈ Focus on high-priority risks that have the greatest potential to disrupt trading activities or result in significant financial losses.

e. Risk Tolerance:

◈ Establish risk tolerance levels for different types of risks. Determine how much risk is acceptable within the risk management framework.

f. Risk Mitigation and Management:

◈ Develop risk mitigation strategies and risk management plans for identified risks.

◈ Consider using hedging instruments, diversification, credit risk mitigation tools, and compliance procedures to manage and mitigate risks.

g. Monitoring and Review:

◈ Continuously monitor and review risks to ensure that risk management strategies remain effective.

◈ Adjust risk management approaches as market conditions and risk profiles change.

Effective risk identification and assessment are ongoing processes in commodity trading. By regularly evaluating and updating risk profiles, traders and investors can adapt to changing market conditions and improve their overall risk management practices.

Risk mitigation techniques are essential tools for managing the various risks associated with commodity trading. These techniques help traders, investors, and businesses protect their positions and assets from adverse market movements and other potential challenges. Here are some commonly used risk mitigation techniques in commodity trading:

1. Hedging:

Hedging is a fundamental risk mitigation strategy in commodity trading. It involves taking an offsetting position in a derivative contract to protect against the risk of adverse price movements in the underlying commodity. There are two primary types of hedges:

◈ **Long Hedge**: Used by producers or consumers of commodities to lock in a favorable price. For example, a farmer might use a long hedge to secure a minimum price for their crop before harvest.

◈ **Short Hedge**: Used by traders or businesses to protect against rising prices. For instance, an airline might use a short hedge to lock in fuel prices to mitigate the risk of rising jet fuel costs.

Hedging can be accomplished using futures contracts, options contracts, or swaps, depending on the specific risk exposure and objectives.

2. Options Contracts:

Options provide traders and businesses with the right (but not the obligation) to buy (call option) or sell (put option) a commodity at a predetermined price (strike price) before or on a specified future date. Options can be used for risk mitigation in several ways:

◈ **Protective Put**: A protective put option can be purchased to limit potential losses on a long commodity position by allowing the holder to sell the commodity at the strike price, protecting against price declines.

◈ **Covered Call**: A covered call strategy involves selling call options on a commodity that the trader already owns. It generates income but limits potential gains if prices rise above the strike price.

◈ **Collars**: A collar strategy combines the purchase of a protective put and the sale of a covered call to establish a price range within which the commodity's price can fluctuate without significant gain or loss.

Options provide flexibility in tailoring risk management strategies to specific risk profiles and market conditions.

3. Diversification:

Diversification is a risk mitigation technique that involves spreading investments across a variety of commodities or asset classes. By diversifying, traders and investors reduce the impact of adverse price movements in any single commodity. Key aspects of diversification include:

◈ **Commodity Selection**: Diversify across different commodities, such as agricultural, energy, metals, and soft commodities, to reduce concentration risk.

◈ **Asset Allocation**: Allocate assets to a mix of commodities, equities, fixed income, and other asset classes to balance risk and return.

◈ **Geographic Diversification**: Invest in commodities from different regions to reduce exposure to geopolitical and regional risks.

◈ **Time Horizon**: Consider long-term and short-term investment horizons to align diversification strategies with specific goals.

Diversification can help stabilize a portfolio's performance and reduce the impact of price volatility in individual commodities.

4. Physical Storage and Inventory Management:

For participants involved in physical commodity trading, proper storage and inventory management are essential risk mitigation techniques. Efficient storage facilities, quality control measures, and inventory management strategies can help safeguard physical commodities from spoilage, theft, or degradation, reducing operational and price risk.

5. Risk Monitoring and Analysis:

Regularly monitoring and analyzing market and portfolio risks are essential components of risk mitigation. Traders and investors use risk management tools and software to assess risk exposures, stress test scenarios, and evaluate the effectiveness of hedging strategies.

6. Compliance and Regulatory Adherence:

Compliance with relevant regulations and adherence to risk management policies and procedures are crucial for mitigating regulatory and compliance risks. Staying informed about changing regulations and industry best practices is essential.

Successful risk mitigation in commodity trading often involves a combination of these techniques tailored to specific objectives and market conditions. The choice of risk mitigation strategies depends on factors such as risk tolerance, investment horizon, and the nature of the commodities being traded. Additionally, risk mitigation should be an ongoing process, adapting to changing market dynamics and risk profiles.

Risk management policies play a pivotal role in commodity trading and are essential for ensuring the systematic and effective management of various risks that traders, investors, and businesses encounter. These policies provide a framework for identifying, assessing, and mitigating risks, and they help establish guidelines and procedures for risk management practices. Here's an overview of the role and importance of risk management policies in commodity trading:

1. Define Risk Tolerance:

⟐ Risk management policies set the acceptable level of risk or risk tolerance for a trading or investment operation. This threshold is based on the organization's financial goals, risk appetite, and overall strategy.

⟐ It helps determine how much risk an entity is willing to assume and under what conditions risk mitigation measures should be activated.

2. Identify and Assess Risks:

⟐ Risk management policies outline the process for identifying and assessing various types of risks, including price risk, credit risk, operational risk, regulatory risk, and others.

◈ They define the tools, models, and methodologies to be used in risk assessment, allowing for a systematic analysis of risk exposure.

3. Mitigate and Manage Risks:

◈ Risk management policies provide guidance on how to mitigate and manage identified risks. This includes the use of hedging strategies, options contracts, diversification, and other risk mitigation techniques.

◈ Policies may specify the circumstances under which risk mitigation measures should be employed and the responsibilities of individuals or teams in executing these measures.

4. Establish Reporting and Monitoring Mechanisms:

◈ Policies set forth reporting requirements and monitoring mechanisms to ensure that risk exposures are regularly assessed and reviewed.

◈ They define the frequency and format of risk reports, including key risk indicators (KRIs) and other metrics.

5. Compliance and Regulatory Adherence:

◈ Risk management policies help ensure compliance with relevant regulations and industry standards. They specify the procedures and controls needed to meet regulatory requirements.

◈ Compliance with risk management policies is crucial to avoiding legal and regulatory issues.

6. Contingency Planning:

◈ Policies may include contingency and crisis management plans to address unexpected events, such as natural disasters, geopolitical crises, or extreme market volatility.

◈ Contingency plans outline how to respond to emergencies and protect assets and positions.

7. Consistency and Transparency:

◈ Risk management policies promote consistency and transparency in decision-making processes. They help ensure that risk assessment and mitigation strategies are consistently applied across the organization.

◈ Transparency is crucial for stakeholders, including investors, partners, and regulatory authorities, who need to understand how risks are managed.

8. Continuous Improvement:

◈ Risk management policies should be adaptable and subject to periodic reviews and updates. As market conditions change and new risks emerge, policies need to evolve to address these challenges effectively.

9. Training and Education:

◈ Policies may include provisions for training and educating employees and stakeholders on risk management practices, procedures, and the importance of risk awareness.

10. Documentation and Record Keeping:

◈ Comprehensive documentation and record-keeping practices are often mandated by risk management policies. Proper records help in auditing and assessing the effectiveness of risk management efforts.

In essence, risk management policies serve as a roadmap for navigating the complex landscape of commodity trading. They provide structure, discipline, and consistency in addressing risks, which is crucial for achieving financial goals while safeguarding against unexpected events and market fluctuations. Successful commodity trading operations prioritize the development, implementation, and adherence to well-defined risk management policies.

Chapter 6: Commodity Price Forecasting

Methods of Price Forecasting (Time Series Analysis, Econometric Models)

Commodity price forecasting is a crucial aspect of commodity trading and investment, as it helps market participants make informed decisions. Various methods and techniques are used for forecasting commodity prices, depending on data availability, market conditions, and the specific commodity being analyzed. Two commonly used methods are time series analysis and econometric models:

a. Time Series Analysis:

Time series analysis involves studying historical price data to identify patterns, trends, and relationships within a commodity's price history. Here are some key components of time series analysis for commodity price forecasting:

◈ **Moving Averages:** Moving averages, such as the simple moving average (SMA) and exponential moving average (EMA), smooth out price data over a specified time period. Traders often use moving averages to identify trends and potential trend reversals.

◈ **Seasonal Decomposition:** Time series data often exhibit seasonal patterns due to factors like weather, holidays, or annual production cycles. Seasonal decomposition separates these components from the overall trend, making it easier to forecast future prices.

◈ **Autoregressive Integrated Moving Average (ARIMA):** ARIMA models are a class of statistical models used to capture time series data's autocorrelation and seasonality. They are especially useful for forecasting when the data exhibit non-stationarity (i.e., when statistical properties change over time).

◈ **GARCH Models:** Generalized Autoregressive Conditional Heteroskedasticity (GARCH) models are used to analyze and forecast volatility in commodity prices. GARCH models account for time-varying volatility, which is common in financial and commodity markets.

◈ **Cointegration and Error Correction Models:** Cointegration tests assess the long-term equilibrium relationships between commodities and related assets. Error correction models adjust for short-term deviations from this equilibrium, aiding in price forecasting.

Time series analysis is particularly useful for short to medium-term price forecasting and is based on historical price patterns and statistical methods.

b. Econometric Models:

Econometric models incorporate economic theories and relationships to forecast commodity prices. These models consider various fundamental factors that can influence prices. Here are some common econometric models used in commodity price forecasting:

◈ **Supply and Demand Models:** These models analyze the balance between supply and demand factors for a specific commodity. Factors like production, consumption, inventories, and external influences are considered to forecast price movements.

◈ **Granger Causality Models:** Granger causality tests examine whether past values of one or more variables can predict future values of another variable. This can help identify causal relationships between economic variables and commodity prices.

◈ **Vector Autoregression (VAR):** VAR models are used to analyze the joint dynamics of multiple economic variables and their impact on commodity prices. They are useful for capturing interdependencies between different markets and factors.

◈ **Machine Learning and Artificial Intelligence:** Advanced techniques like machine learning and artificial intelligence (AI) are increasingly used for price forecasting. Algorithms like neural networks and support vector machines can analyze large datasets and identify complex patterns.

◈ **Time-Varying Parameter Models:** These models allow parameters to change over time, reflecting evolving economic conditions and relationships. They are well-suited for capturing changing market dynamics.

Econometric models are often used for longer-term price forecasting and can incorporate a wide range of economic and financial variables into the analysis.

In practice, many analysts and traders use a combination of time series analysis, econometric models, and qualitative analysis to make more accurate price forecasts. Additionally, the choice of forecasting method may depend on the specific commodity's characteristics, market conditions, and the available data.

In commodity price forecasting, multiple factors influence and drive price movements. These factors can be broadly categorized into three main categories: supply, demand, and macro-economic indicators. Analyzing these factors helps traders, investors, and analysts make informed forecasts. Here's an overview of each category:

1. Supply Factors:

Supply factors pertain to the production and availability of a commodity. Changes in supply can significantly impact commodity prices. Key supply-related factors to consider in forecasting include:

◈ **Production Levels**: The quantity of a commodity produced globally or in specific regions is a critical factor. Events affecting production, such as crop yields for agricultural commodities or drilling activity for energy commodities, can have a substantial impact.

◈ **Weather and Climate**: Weather conditions, including temperature, precipitation, and natural disasters like droughts or hurricanes, can affect agricultural and energy commodities. Weather-related risks can lead to supply disruptions.

◈ **Geopolitical Events**: Political instability, trade disputes, sanctions, and conflicts in major commodity-producing regions can disrupt supply chains and reduce the availability of certain commodities.

◈ **Technological Advancements**: Technological innovations can influence supply by improving production efficiency or unlocking new sources of supply, such as shale oil and gas extraction technologies.

◈ **Regulations and Environmental Policies**: Regulations governing resource extraction, emissions, and environmental protections can impact the supply of certain commodities. Changes in these policies can affect production costs and supply levels.

2. Demand Factors:

Demand factors focus on the consumption and utilization of commodities. Changes in demand can influence commodity prices. Key demand-related factors to consider in forecasting include:

◈ **Economic Growth**: The overall economic health of countries and regions affects demand for commodities. Strong economic growth often leads to increased consumption of energy and industrial commodities.

◈ **Population Growth**: Rising populations can drive increased demand for agricultural commodities to meet food and fiber needs.

◈ **Consumer Behavior**: Consumer preferences, dietary habits, and lifestyle changes can affect demand for specific agricultural products, such as organic or plant-based foods.

◈ **Industrial and Technological Trends**: Advancements in technology, including the growth of electric vehicles, renewable energy, and electronics manufacturing, impact demand for specific metals and minerals.

◈ **Government Policies**: Policies related to infrastructure development, energy transition, and subsidies can influence demand for specific commodities. For example, government incentives for renewable energy adoption can boost demand for solar panels and wind turbines.

3. Macro-Economic Indicators:

Macro-economic indicators provide insights into broader economic conditions that can indirectly affect commodity prices. These indicators help analysts gauge the overall economic environment, which can impact supply and demand. Key macro-economic indicators include:

◈ **Interest Rates**: Central bank interest rate policies can influence investment flows, impacting financial markets and commodity prices.

◈ **Inflation**: High inflation rates may lead investors to seek commodities as a hedge against currency devaluation, potentially driving up commodity prices.

◈ **Currency Exchange Rates**: Currency fluctuations can affect the competitiveness of commodity exports and imports, influencing supply and demand dynamics.

◈ **Global Economic Trends**: Economic indicators like GDP growth, consumer sentiment, and manufacturing activity provide insights into overall economic conditions and their impact on commodity demand.

◈ **Monetary Policies**: The use of monetary tools, such as quantitative easing or tightening, can affect liquidity and asset prices, including commodities.

◈ **Trade Policies**: International trade policies, tariffs, and trade agreements can influence the flow of commodities between countries, affecting supply and demand balances.

Effective commodity price forecasting involves analyzing a combination of these supply, demand, and macro-economic factors. Moreover, it requires monitoring news, market sentiment, and geopolitical developments, as these can create sudden shifts in commodity markets. Analysts use a variety of tools and models to incorporate these factors into their forecasts and make informed trading and investment decisions.

Scenario analysis and sensitivity testing are valuable techniques used in commodity price forecasting and risk management to assess how changes in various factors can impact outcomes, particularly in uncertain or volatile environments. These techniques help traders, investors, and businesses understand the range of potential outcomes and make informed decisions. Here's an overview of scenario analysis and sensitivity testing:

Scenario Analysis:

Scenario analysis involves creating multiple scenarios or hypothetical situations that reflect different future states of the world, including changes in key variables and market conditions. Each scenario represents a plausible set of circumstances and outcomes. The purpose of scenario analysis in commodity price forecasting is to:

◈ **Identify Risks and Opportunities**: Scenario analysis helps identify potential risks and opportunities associated with different market conditions. By exploring a range of scenarios, participants can be better prepared for various outcomes.

◈ **Assess Impact**: Analysts assess how each scenario would impact commodity prices, supply and demand dynamics, and financial performance. This allows for a more comprehensive understanding of the potential consequences of different scenarios.

◈ **Quantify Risk Exposure**: Scenario analysis quantifies the potential financial impact of each scenario, helping traders and investors assess their exposure to different risk factors.

◈ **Strategic Planning**: Scenario analysis assists in strategic planning by allowing organizations to develop contingency plans and risk mitigation strategies tailored to specific scenarios.

Steps in Scenario Analysis:

1. **Identification of Key Variables**: Start by identifying the critical variables and factors that can influence commodity prices and market conditions. These variables may include supply, demand, economic indicators, geopolitical events, and regulatory changes.

2. **Define Scenarios**: Create a set of scenarios that represent different future states. Scenarios should be plausible and capture a range of potential outcomes. For example, scenarios could include a base case, a bullish case, and a bearish case.

3. **Quantify Assumptions**: Assign specific values or assumptions to the key variables for each scenario. These values should reflect the conditions and factors relevant to the scenario.

4. **Analyze Impact**: Use quantitative models or analyses to assess how each scenario would impact commodity prices, supply-demand balances, and financial metrics. Consider both short-term and long-term effects.

5. **Evaluate Risk Exposure**: Calculate the financial impact or risk exposure associated with each scenario. This may involve estimating potential losses or gains.

6. **Strategic Planning**: Develop strategies and contingency plans based on the outcomes of scenario analysis. Determine how to respond if specific scenarios materialize.

Sensitivity Testing:

Sensitivity testing, also known as sensitivity analysis, focuses on assessing how variations in a single variable or assumption affect the outcome or output of a model or forecast. In commodity price forecasting, sensitivity testing helps to:

- **Identify Key Drivers**: Identify which variables or assumptions have the most significant impact on commodity price forecasts and risk exposure.

- **Quantify Sensitivity**: Measure how sensitive price forecasts or financial metrics are to changes in specific variables. This quantification helps assess risk exposure.

- **Scenario Refinement**: Use sensitivity testing results to refine and adjust scenarios in scenario analysis. It provides insights into which variables should be varied in different scenarios.

Steps in Sensitivity Testing:

1. **Select Variable**: Choose the variable or assumption that you want to test for sensitivity. This variable is typically a critical driver of commodity prices, such as oil demand or weather patterns.

2. **Define Range**: Specify a range or set of values for the selected variable. This range should cover plausible variations or scenarios.

3. **Analyze Impact**: Run the model or forecast with different values of the selected variable. Observe how changes in the variable impact commodity price forecasts or risk exposure.

4. **Quantify Sensitivity**: Calculate and quantify the sensitivity of the forecasted outcomes to changes in the selected variable. This can be expressed as a sensitivity coefficient or percentage change.

Scenario analysis and sensitivity testing are essential tools for assessing and managing risk in commodity trading and investment. They provide valuable insights into the potential impact of various market conditions and help market participants make informed decisions and develop robust risk management strategies.

Real-life case studies in price forecasting provide practical insights into the challenges and strategies involved in predicting commodity prices. These cases highlight the importance of understanding market dynamics, conducting thorough analysis, and adapting to changing conditions. Here are a few notable case studies:

1. Oil Price Collapse (2014-2016):

◈ **Background:** One of the most significant commodity price events in recent history was the sharp decline in oil prices that began in mid-2014. Prices plummeted from over $100 per barrel to below $30 per barrel by early 2016. This collapse had far-reaching consequences for oil-producing countries, energy companies, and global financial markets.

◈ **Forecasting Challenge:** Many analysts and institutions failed to predict the magnitude of the oil price decline. Forecasters faced challenges in anticipating the oversupply of oil due to increased production, weaker demand growth, and OPEC's decision to maintain high production levels.

◈ **Key Takeaways:** This case underscores the importance of considering both supply and demand dynamics in commodity price forecasting. It also highlights the influence of geopolitical factors and production decisions by major producers.

2. Soybean Price Volatility (2019-2020):

◈ **Background:** Soybean prices experienced significant volatility during the trade tensions between the United States and China in 2019 and 2020. The dispute led to tariffs on U.S. soybean exports to China, affecting global soybean markets.

◈ **Forecasting Challenge:** Forecasting soybean prices during this period was challenging due to the uncertainty surrounding trade negotiations, shifts in demand patterns, and supply disruptions caused by weather events. Analysts had to consider both trade policy developments and traditional supply-demand fundamentals.

◈ **Key Takeaways:** This case illustrates the impact of geopolitical events on commodity markets and the need to integrate policy analysis into price forecasts. It also highlights the importance of monitoring global trade dynamics for commodities with significant export dependencies.

3. Gold Price Surge (2020-2021):

◈ **Background:** The price of gold experienced a significant rally in 2020 and early 2021, reaching record highs above $2,000 per ounce. This surge was driven by factors such as economic uncertainty, low-interest rates, and increased demand for safe-haven assets during the COVID-19 pandemic.

◈ **Forecasting Challenge:** Forecasting the gold price during this period required consideration of macroeconomic factors, including monetary policy, inflation expectations, and market sentiment. Analysts had to adapt to changing economic conditions and investor behavior.

◈ **Key Takeaways:** This case underscores the importance of understanding the broader economic and financial context when forecasting commodity prices. It also highlights the role of investor sentiment and financial market conditions in shaping commodity price trends.

4. Natural Gas Price Fluctuations (Various Periods):

◈ **Background:** Natural gas prices are known for their volatility, influenced by factors such as weather patterns, supply and demand imbalances, and storage levels. Numerous cases highlight the challenges of forecasting natural gas prices for energy companies and traders.

◈ **Forecasting Challenge:** Forecasting natural gas prices requires monitoring weather forecasts, production levels, storage capacity, and demand trends. Weather events like polar vortexes can lead to sudden and significant price spikes.

◈ **Key Takeaways:** The natural gas market demonstrates the importance of real-time data, robust supply-demand analysis, and understanding the impact of weather on commodity prices. It also emphasizes the need for hedging strategies to mitigate price risk.

These real-life case studies in price forecasting underscore the complexity of commodity markets and the need for a holistic approach to analysis. Successful forecasting often involves a combination of fundamental analysis, geopolitical awareness, and an understanding of market sentiment. Additionally, market participants must continuously adapt their forecasting methods in response to changing conditions and emerging risks.

Chapter 7: Commodity Trading and Regulation

Regulatory Framework for Commodity Trading

Commodity trading is subject to various regulatory frameworks at both national and international levels. These regulations aim to ensure fair, transparent, and efficient markets while mitigating risks for market participants. The specific regulatory framework for commodity trading can vary from one country or region to another, but there are common elements and key principles that guide regulation in this sector. Here are some essential components of the regulatory framework for commodity trading:

a. Regulatory Agencies:

◈ **Commodity Futures Trading Commission (CFTC, United States):** In the United States, the CFTC is the primary regulatory authority overseeing commodity futures and options markets. It regulates commodity exchanges, ensures market integrity, and enforces rules to protect market participants.

◈ **Securities and Exchange Commission (SEC, United States):** The SEC regulates some aspects of commodity trading, particularly those related to exchange-traded funds (ETFs) and securities tied to commodities.

◈ **Financial Conduct Authority (FCA, United Kingdom):** The FCA oversees commodity derivative markets in the UK and enforces regulations to maintain market integrity and protect consumers.

◈ **European Securities and Markets Authority (ESMA):** ESMA plays a coordinating role in regulating commodity markets across

European Union (EU) member states, ensuring consistency in regulatory standards.

⟐ **International Organizations:** Organizations like the International Organization of Securities Commissions (IOSCO) provide global guidance on best practices and principles for commodity market regulation.

b. Exchange Regulations:

⟐ **Commodity Exchanges:** Commodity futures and options trading typically occur on regulated exchanges, such as the Chicago Mercantile Exchange (CME) or the Intercontinental Exchange (ICE). These exchanges have their own rules and regulations that traders must adhere to.

⟐ **Market Surveillance:** Exchanges often employ surveillance mechanisms to monitor trading activities and detect irregularities, market manipulation, or abusive trading practices.

c. Market Integrity:

⟐ **Anti-Manipulation and Fraud Regulations:** Regulations are in place to prevent market manipulation, fraud, and abusive trading practices that can distort commodity prices.

⟐ **Market Transparency:** Transparency requirements ensure that price and trading information is readily accessible to market participants and the public.

d. Position Limits:

⟐ **Position Limits:** Regulatory authorities may impose position limits to prevent a single trader or entity from acquiring excessive positions in commodity futures contracts, which can distort supply and demand dynamics.

e. Risk Management:

◈ **Margin Requirements:** Margin requirements dictate the amount of collateral that traders must maintain to cover potential losses. They help manage counterparty risk.

◈ **Clearinghouses:** Central clearinghouses play a crucial role in managing counterparty risk by acting as intermediaries between buyers and sellers, guaranteeing the performance of trades.

f. Consumer Protection:

◈ **Disclosure and Reporting:** Regulations often require disclosures and reporting of positions and trading activities, promoting transparency and accountability.

◈ **Investor Education:** Regulatory authorities may encourage investor education initiatives to ensure that participants understand the risks and complexities of commodity trading.

g. Environmental and Sustainability Regulations:

◈ **Environmental Regulations:** For commodities like energy, metals, and agriculture, environmental regulations may impact production, transportation, and supply, which can influence commodity prices.

h. International Agreements:

◈ **International Trade Agreements:** International agreements, such as those under the World Trade Organization (WTO), can affect the cross-border trading of commodities and impact market access and tariffs.

◈ **Commodity-Specific Agreements:** Some commodities, like oil, have specific international agreements that govern production, pricing, and trade, such as OPEC agreements.

It's important to note that regulations may evolve over time in response to changing market conditions and emerging risks. Commodity traders, investors, and businesses engaged in commodity markets must stay informed about regulatory changes and ensure compliance to operate legally and responsibly. Additionally, market participants often use risk management strategies, including hedging and diversification, to navigate regulatory compliance and associated risks.

Market manipulation and insider trading are illegal activities that can undermine the integrity and fairness of commodity markets. Regulators and exchanges have strict rules and regulations in place to detect, prevent, and penalize these activities. Here's an overview of market manipulation and insider trading in the context of commodity trading:

1. Market Manipulation:

Market manipulation refers to actions taken by traders or entities with the intent to artificially influence commodity prices, supply and demand dynamics, or trading activity. It can distort market prices, create false or misleading impressions, and harm other market participants. Common forms of market manipulation include:

◈ **Price Rigging:** Attempts to control or manipulate the price of a commodity by engaging in coordinated buying or selling activities.

◈ **Spoofing:** Placing orders with the intent to cancel them before execution to create a false impression of market demand or supply.

◈ **Front-Running:** Executing trades on advance knowledge of a large order that will influence the market, profiting from the expected price movement.

◈ **Cornering the Market:** Accumulating a dominant position in a commodity with the intent to control supply and manipulate prices.

◈ **Churning:** Excessive trading in an account to generate commissions for a broker, often at the expense of the client.

◈ **Pump and Dump:** Promoting a commodity's price through false or exaggerated information and then selling off the accumulated position at the inflated price.

◈ **Wash Trading:** Simultaneously buying and selling the same commodity to create the appearance of trading activity, with no change in ownership.

Regulatory authorities, such as the CFTC and SEC in the United States, actively monitor and investigate suspected cases of market manipulation. Violators can face severe penalties, including fines, trading bans, and even criminal charges.

2. Insider Trading:

Insider trading occurs when individuals or entities with access to non-public, material information about a commodity or a company engaged in commodity trading use that information for personal gain or to benefit others. Insider trading can distort the fairness of the market and harm other traders who do not have access to the same information. Key points related to insider trading include:

◈ **Material Non-Public Information (MNPI):** Insider trading involves trading based on MNPI, which includes information that, if disclosed, could reasonably be expected to affect the price of a commodity.

◈ **Types of Insiders:** Insiders can include corporate officers, directors, employees, and anyone with access to MNPI through their relationship with a company, including analysts, consultants, and contractors.

◈ **Legal and Illegal Insider Trading:** Legal insider trading occurs when insiders buy or sell shares of their own company's stock but report the transactions to the relevant regulatory authorities. Illegal insider trading occurs when MNPI is used for trading without proper disclosure.

◈ **Tipper and Tippee Liability:** Liability for insider trading can extend to individuals who receive MNPI from an insider (the tipper) and use it to trade (the tippee).

◈ **Enforcement:** Regulatory bodies and law enforcement agencies actively investigate and prosecute cases of insider trading. Penalties can include fines, imprisonment, and civil actions.

Commodity trading firms and participants must have strong compliance and monitoring mechanisms in place to prevent and detect market manipulation and insider trading. Additionally, they are often required to report suspicious activities to regulatory authorities to help maintain market integrity and transparency. Commodity traders should also be aware of the specific rules and regulations governing their markets and regions to ensure compliance.

Reporting and compliance requirements in commodity trading are essential to ensure the transparency, integrity, and fairness of the markets. Regulatory authorities impose specific obligations on market participants to monitor and report their activities, maintain proper records, and adhere to trading rules. Here are some common reporting and compliance requirements in commodity trading:

1. Transaction Reporting:

◈ **Trade Confirmation:** Traders are often required to promptly confirm their trades with counterparties. These confirmations should include details such as trade date, quantity, price, and other relevant terms.

◈ **Regulatory Reporting:** Depending on the jurisdiction and type of commodity, traders may be obligated to report their trades to regulatory authorities. This reporting helps regulators monitor market activity and detect potential irregularities or violations.

2. Position Reporting:

◈ **Position Limits:** Regulators may impose position limits on the maximum number of contracts or units of a commodity that a trader or entity can hold. Traders are required to monitor and report their positions to ensure compliance with these limits.

◈ **Large Trader Reporting:** Traders who exceed certain thresholds may be classified as large traders and are required to report their positions to regulators. This reporting helps regulators identify traders with significant market influence.

3. Compliance with Trading Rules:

◈ **Market Rules and Exchange Regulations:** Traders must adhere to the rules and regulations of the commodity exchange on which they operate. These rules cover trading hours, order types, margin requirements, and other trading practices.

◈ **Anti-Manipulation and Fraud Prohibitions:** Traders must not engage in market manipulation, fraud, or deceptive practices. Compliance with anti-manipulation rules is crucial to maintaining market integrity.

4. Risk Management:

◈ **Margin Requirements:** Traders are typically required to maintain margin accounts to cover potential losses. They must comply with margin calls and meet margin requirements set by exchanges and clearinghouses.

5. Recordkeeping:

◈ **Trade Records:** Traders must maintain detailed records of their trading activities, including order execution, trade confirmations, and communication related to trades. These records should be retained for a specified period and made available for regulatory audits.

6. Reporting of Suspicious Activities:

◈ **Whistleblower Programs:** Some regulatory authorities provide whistleblower programs that allow individuals to report suspicious or illegal activities without fear of retaliation. Encouraging internal reporting is also a compliance requirement for some firms.

7. Regulatory Filings and Disclosures:

◈ **Financial Reporting:** Publicly traded commodity-related companies may be required to file financial reports and disclosures with regulatory authorities, including the SEC in the United States.

◈ **Compliance Reports:** Some regulators require periodic compliance reports from trading firms, detailing their adherence to trading and risk management rules.

8. Cross-Border and International Compliance:

◈ **Cross-Border Trading:** For global commodity trading, firms must comply with regulations in multiple jurisdictions when trading across borders. This includes adhering to the regulations of both the home country and the foreign country where trading occurs.

9. Environmental and Sustainability Reporting:

◈ **Environmental Regulations:** In the case of energy commodities and other commodities with environmental impacts, firms may be required to report on emissions, environmental compliance, and sustainability practices.

10. Market Abuse and Insider Trading Reporting:

◈ **Suspicious Activity Reporting:** Firms are often obligated to report any suspicious trading activity, market manipulation, or insider trading to the relevant regulatory authorities.

It's important for market participants to have robust compliance programs and systems in place to ensure that they meet these reporting and compliance requirements. Failure to comply with these obligations can result in fines, penalties, trading suspensions, or other regulatory actions that can adversely affect a trader's reputation and business operations. Additionally, compliance requirements can vary by jurisdiction and may change over time, so traders and firms must stay informed about relevant regulations and updates.

Regulatory authorities play a crucial role in the oversight and supervision of commodity markets. Their primary mission is to ensure the fairness, transparency, integrity, and stability of these markets while protecting the interests of market participants and the public. The specific roles and responsibilities of regulatory authorities in commodity trading include:

1. Rule-Making and Oversight:

◈ **Establishing Rules:** Regulatory authorities create and enforce rules and regulations governing commodity trading. These rules cover areas such as market conduct, trading practices, position limits, and reporting requirements.

◈ **Market Surveillance:** Regulatory authorities monitor trading activity to detect and investigate market manipulation, insider trading, and other irregularities. They use advanced surveillance technologies and data analysis to identify suspicious trading patterns.

2. Licensing and Registration:

◈ **Market Participants:** Regulatory authorities may require individuals and entities engaged in commodity trading, including traders, brokers, exchanges, and clearinghouses, to obtain licenses or register with the regulatory agency.

3. Market Integrity and Transparency:

◈ **Enforcing Fair Practices:** Regulatory authorities enforce rules that promote fair trading practices, such as preventing market manipulation, price rigging, and fraudulent activities.

◈ **Transparency:** They ensure that price and trading information is readily accessible to market participants and the public. This transparency helps maintain market confidence.

4. Position Limits and Accountability:

◈ **Position Limits:** Regulators may impose position limits to prevent traders from acquiring excessively large positions that could distort market dynamics. They monitor and enforce these limits.

◈ **Large Trader Reporting:** Regulators may require large traders to report their positions to prevent market concentration and maintain market stability.

5. Risk Management:

◈ **Margin Requirements:** Regulatory authorities set and enforce margin requirements to ensure that traders maintain sufficient collateral to cover potential losses. These requirements help manage counterparty risk.

◈ **Central Clearinghouses:** They oversee central clearinghouses, which act as intermediaries in trades, ensuring the fulfillment of contracts and reducing counterparty risk.

6. Investor Protection:

◈ **Disclosure and Reporting:** Regulatory authorities may require public companies engaged in commodity-related activities to disclose material information to investors, enhancing investor protection.

7. Market Data and Reporting:

◈ **Regulatory Reporting:** Regulatory authorities often require traders and firms to report their trading activities and positions. These reports help regulators monitor market activity and assess compliance.

◈ **Market Data Collection:** They collect and disseminate market data, including prices, trading volumes, and open interest, to market participants and the public.

8. Investigations and Enforcement:

◈ **Investigating Violations:** Regulatory authorities investigate alleged violations of commodity trading rules and regulations. They have the authority to conduct audits and inspections of trading firms.

◈ **Enforcement Actions:** In response to violations, regulatory authorities may take enforcement actions, including imposing fines, penalties, trading suspensions, or revoking licenses.

9. International Coordination:

◈ **Collaboration:** Regulatory authorities often collaborate with international counterparts to ensure consistency in global commodity trading regulations and to address cross-border trading challenges.

◈ **Standardization:** They work with international organizations to develop and promote global standards for commodity market regulation.

10. Crisis Management:

◈ **Contingency Planning:** Regulatory authorities may develop contingency plans and crisis management procedures to address market disruptions or extraordinary events.

◈ **Market Stabilization:** In times of crisis, they may take measures to stabilize markets, such as implementing trading halts or circuit breakers.

11. Education and Outreach:

◈ **Investor Education:** Some regulatory authorities engage in investor education and outreach initiatives to help the public understand the risks and complexities of commodity trading.

Overall, regulatory authorities are essential to maintaining market integrity, protecting participants, and ensuring the proper functioning of commodity markets. They adapt to evolving market conditions, technological changes, and emerging risks to fulfill their roles effectively. Market participants, including traders, brokers, and exchanges, must comply with the regulations set forth by these authorities to operate legally and responsibly in the commodity trading sector.

Chapter 8: Commodity Trading and Sustainability

Sustainable Practices in Commodity Trading

Sustainability has become a critical consideration in commodity trading due to increasing global awareness of environmental and social issues. Sustainable practices in commodity trading aim to minimize negative impacts on the environment, promote social responsibility, and ensure the long-term viability of commodity production and trade. Here are key sustainable practices in commodity trading:

a. Environmental Sustainability:

1. **Responsible Sourcing:** Traders strive to source commodities, such as agricultural products, minerals, and energy resources, from suppliers and producers who adhere to environmentally responsible practices. This includes efforts to reduce deforestation, protect biodiversity, and limit carbon emissions.

2. **Certification Programs:** Some commodities have certification programs (e.g., Fair Trade, Rainforest Alliance) that promote environmentally sustainable and socially responsible production. Traders may support and promote certified commodities.

3. **Environmental Impact Assessment:** Before engaging in commodity extraction or production, traders conduct environmental impact assessments to understand and mitigate potential negative effects on ecosystems and natural resources.

4. **Resource Efficiency:** Traders and producers work to optimize resource use, minimize waste, and reduce energy consumption throughout the commodity supply chain.

b. Social Responsibility:

1. **Labor Standards:** Traders adhere to fair labor practices and ensure that workers along the supply chain are treated ethically and receive fair wages and safe working conditions.

2. **Community Engagement:** Traders engage with local communities near commodity production sites, addressing community concerns, and investing in social development initiatives.

3. **Supply Chain Transparency:** Transparency initiatives help trace the origins of commodities and ensure that they are not linked to human rights abuses, child labor, or unethical practices.

4. **Conflict Minerals**: In the case of minerals like gold, tin, tantalum, and tungsten, traders must comply with regulations aimed at preventing the trade of minerals that finance armed conflict and human rights violations (e.g., the Dodd-Frank Act in the U.S.).

c. Risk Mitigation:

1. **Climate Risk Assessment:** Traders assess climate-related risks, such as extreme weather events or changing regulatory frameworks, that could impact commodity production, supply, and demand.

2. **Diversification:** Diversifying commodity portfolios can help traders mitigate risks associated with the fluctuation of commodity prices and supply disruptions.

d. Sustainable Finance:

1. **Green Finance:** Traders may seek funding or invest in projects that align with environmental sustainability goals, such as renewable energy projects or sustainable agriculture initiatives.

2. **Environmental, Social, and Governance (ESG) Criteria:** Investors and traders incorporate ESG criteria into their decision-making processes, evaluating companies based on their environmental, social, and governance practices.

e. Technological Innovation:

1. **Blockchain Technology:** Some commodity traders use blockchain technology to enhance transparency and traceability throughout the supply chain, ensuring that sustainable practices are followed.

2. **Data Analytics:** Advanced data analytics enable traders to better understand and optimize supply chain efficiency, reducing waste and emissions.

3. **Remote Sensing:** Satellite imagery and remote sensing technologies are used to monitor land use changes and deforestation, particularly in the context of agricultural commodities.

f. Regulatory Compliance:

1. **Compliance with Environmental Regulations:** Traders must comply with local and international environmental regulations related to commodity production, transportation, and emissions.

2. **Disclosure and Reporting:** Some regulatory authorities require traders to disclose their sustainability efforts and report on their environmental and social performance.

Incorporating sustainable practices in commodity trading is not only driven by ethical considerations but also by the increasing demand from consumers, investors, and regulators for responsible and environmentally friendly products. Sustainable commodity trading helps mitigate risks, enhance market reputation, and contribute to a more environmentally and socially responsible global economy.

ESG (Environmental, Social, and Governance) considerations have gained significant importance in commodity investments as investors increasingly prioritize sustainable and responsible investment strategies. ESG factors play a crucial role in shaping investment decisions across various asset classes, including commodities. Here are key ESG considerations in commodity investments:

1. Environmental Factors:

a. Carbon Footprint and Emissions:

⟐ **Carbon Intensity:** Investors assess the carbon intensity of commodities, including energy resources like oil and natural gas. Commodities with lower carbon footprints may be favored as part of decarbonization efforts.

⟐ **Emissions Reduction:** Investments may focus on commodities associated with cleaner and more sustainable energy sources, such as renewable energy and natural gas.

b. Land Use and Biodiversity:

⟐ **Deforestation and Land Conversion:** Investors scrutinize commodities like palm oil, soy, and timber to ensure they are produced without causing deforestation or harm to critical ecosystems.

⟐ **Biodiversity Protection:** Investments may consider commodities produced in ways that protect biodiversity and natural habitats.

c. Water Management:

⟐ **Sustainable Water Use:** Commodities like agriculture and textiles are assessed for their responsible water use and management practices.

d. Pollution and Waste:

◈ **Reducing Pollution:** Investors look for commodities and companies that actively reduce pollution and waste generation in their production processes.

2. Social Factors:

a. Labor Practices:

◈ **Fair Labor Practices:** Commodities must be produced in compliance with fair labor standards, including ethical treatment of workers and payment of fair wages.

◈ **Child Labor and Forced Labor:** Investors actively avoid commodities linked to child labor or forced labor practices.

b. Human Rights:

◈ **Human Rights Abuses:** Investments exclude commodities tied to regions or companies with a history of human rights abuses, such as conflict minerals.

c. Community Engagement:

◈ **Community Development:** Investors seek commodities and companies that engage positively with local communities, promote social development, and respect indigenous rights.

d. Health and Safety:

◈ **Worker Safety:** Commodities must be produced with a focus on worker safety and health.

3. Governance Factors:

a. Corporate Governance:

◈ **Transparency:** Companies involved in commodity production or trading must have transparent governance structures and practices.

◈ **Anti-Corruption:** Investors avoid commodities tied to corrupt practices or companies with weak anti-corruption policies.

b. Supply Chain Traceability:

◈ **Traceability:** Investors seek commodities with transparent supply chains that allow for traceability, ensuring that ESG standards are met throughout the production and distribution process.

c. Ethical Leadership:

◈ **Ethical Leadership:** Companies with strong ethical leadership and a commitment to ESG principles are favored by investors.

4. Risk Management:

a. Climate Risks:

◈ **Physical and Transition Risks:** Investors evaluate how commodities and companies manage climate-related risks, including physical risks like extreme weather events and transition risks associated with changing regulations and market preferences.

b. Regulatory Compliance:

◈ **Compliance with Environmental Regulations:** Investments are scrutinized for adherence to environmental regulations, and non-compliance can lead to reputational and financial risks.

5. Reporting and Transparency:

a. ESG Disclosures:

◈ **Disclosure Practices:** Investors prefer commodities and companies that provide comprehensive ESG disclosures, making it easier to assess their sustainability performance.

b. ESG Ratings and Rankings:

◈ **Third-Party Ratings:** Investors rely on third-party ESG ratings and rankings to assess the ESG performance of commodities and companies.

Commodity investors may consider incorporating ESG considerations into their investment strategies through various means, including ESG-focused exchange-traded funds (ETFs), ESG screens, and engagement with commodity producers and traders to encourage sustainable practices.

Ultimately, ESG considerations in commodity investments aim to align investment choices with environmental and social values while managing risks and seeking long-term sustainable returns. As global awareness of ESG issues continues to grow, the integration of these factors into commodity investment decisions is likely to become even more significant.

Ethical sourcing and supply chain management are critical practices in commodity trading and other industries, aimed at ensuring that commodities are produced, processed, and traded in a responsible, sustainable, and ethical manner. These practices address a range of issues, including human rights, environmental sustainability, and social responsibility. Here's an overview of ethical sourcing and supply chain management in commodity trading:

1. Ethical Sourcing:

a. Responsible Procurement:

◈ **Supplier Due Diligence:** Commodity traders conduct thorough due diligence on suppliers to assess their adherence to ethical and sustainability standards. This includes assessing suppliers' labor practices, environmental impact, and social responsibility.

◈ **Supplier Codes of Conduct:** Traders may establish codes of conduct that suppliers must adhere to, outlining specific ethical and sustainability requirements.

b. Traceability:

◈ **Supply Chain Transparency:** Ethical sourcing involves tracking the origins of commodities and ensuring that they come from sources that meet ethical and sustainability criteria. This traceability helps verify the authenticity of claims regarding responsible sourcing.

◈ **Blockchain Technology:** Some traders use blockchain technology to create transparent and immutable records of supply chain transactions, enhancing traceability.

c. Certification and Standards:

◈ **Certification Programs:** Many commodities have established certification programs (e.g., Fair Trade, Rainforest Alliance) that set ethical and sustainability standards for production. Traders may seek commodities with these certifications.

◈ **Compliance with Standards:** Traders must ensure that the commodities they source comply with relevant ethical and sustainability standards, whether those are industry-specific or broader ESG criteria.

d. Conflict Minerals:

◈ **Conflict Minerals Reporting:** In the case of minerals like gold, tin, tantalum, and tungsten, traders are required to comply with regulations (e.g., the Dodd-Frank Act) that aim to prevent the trade of minerals that finance armed conflict and human rights abuses.

2. Supply Chain Management:

a. Responsible Procurement Practices:

◈ **Labor Practices:** Traders and their suppliers must adhere to fair labor practices and ensure that workers are treated ethically and provided with safe working conditions and fair wages.

◈ **Child Labor and Forced Labor:** Supply chains must be free from child labor and forced labor, and traders should actively ensure compliance.

b. Environmental Stewardship:

◈ **Sustainable Practices:** Traders promote environmentally responsible practices in their supply chains, including reducing waste, minimizing resource consumption, and adopting sustainable agricultural and production methods.

◈ **Deforestation-Free Supply Chains:** Traders work to ensure that commodities like palm oil, soy, and timber are produced without causing deforestation or harm to critical ecosystems.

c. Social Responsibility:

◈ **Community Engagement:** Traders engage positively with local communities near commodity production sites, address community concerns, and invest in social development initiatives.

◈ **Human Rights Protection:** Supply chains must respect human rights, particularly in regions where commodities are produced or sourced.

d. Risk Management:

◈ **Risk Assessment:** Traders conduct risk assessments to identify and mitigate risks associated with their supply chains, including risks related to ethics, sustainability, and social responsibility.

e. Transparency and Reporting:

◈ **Disclosure and Reporting:** Traders report on their supply chain practices, sustainability efforts, and ethical sourcing initiatives. Transparency is crucial for stakeholders to assess a company's commitment to ethical sourcing.

Ethical sourcing and supply chain management are not only ethical imperatives but also help mitigate business risks, enhance brand reputation, and meet the demands of increasingly conscientious consumers and investors. Traders and companies involved in commodity trading must prioritize these practices to ensure the responsible and sustainable production and trading of commodities.

Impact investing in commodities refers to the practice of making investments in commodities or commodity-related projects with the dual purpose of generating financial returns while also creating positive social and environmental impacts. Impact investors seek to align their investments with specific environmental, social, and governance (ESG) objectives, alongside financial goals. Here's an overview of impact investing in commodities:

1. Objectives of Impact Investing in Commodities:

◈ **Social and Environmental Impact:** Impact investors aim to address various social and environmental challenges through their investments. This may include reducing carbon emissions, promoting sustainable agricultural practices, supporting fair labor conditions, and more.

◈ **Financial Returns:** While the primary focus is on making a positive impact, impact investors also seek financial returns, which can come from commodity price appreciation, income generation, or other financial mechanisms.

2. Areas of Impact in Commodity Investing:

Impact investments in commodities can target various areas of impact, including:

◈ **Sustainable Agriculture:** Investing in agricultural commodities using sustainable and environmentally friendly practices, such as organic farming, reduced pesticide use, and soil conservation.

◈ **Renewable Energy:** Supporting commodities related to renewable energy sources like wind, solar, and hydropower, with a focus on reducing carbon emissions and increasing energy sustainability.

◈ **Water Conservation:** Investing in commodities that promote responsible water management and conservation, especially in regions facing water scarcity.

◈ **Forest Conservation:** Supporting commodities that contribute to forest conservation and anti-deforestation efforts, such as sustainable timber production or agroforestry.

◈ **Fair Trade and Ethical Practices:** Investing in commodities produced under fair labor conditions and ethical supply chain practices, promoting social equity and responsible production.

3. Investment Vehicles:

Impact investors can access commodities through various investment vehicles:

◈ **Commodity ETFs:** Exchange-traded funds (ETFs) that track sustainable commodity indices or specific commodities that meet impact criteria.

◈ **Private Equity:** Investing directly in commodity-related companies, startups, or projects that align with impact goals.

◈ **Impact Bonds:** Debt instruments issued to finance projects with specific social and environmental objectives related to commodities.

4. Challenges in Impact Investing in Commodities:

◈ **Complexity:** Commodity markets can be complex, and it may be challenging to trace the impact of specific investments directly to positive social or environmental outcomes.

◈ **Price Volatility:** Commodity prices can be highly volatile, which may pose challenges in achieving both financial returns and impact goals.

◈ **Regulatory and Policy Risks:** The impact of investments in commodities can be influenced by changing regulations and government policies related to environmental and social issues.

5. Measurement and Reporting:

To demonstrate the impact of their investments, impact investors often rely on measurement and reporting frameworks. Common frameworks include the United Nations Sustainable Development Goals (SDGs) and the Impact Management Project's Impact Principles.

6. Ethical Considerations:

Impact investors must carefully evaluate the ethical implications of their investments, ensuring that their goals align with their values and principles.

Impact investing in commodities offers an avenue for investors to support sustainable and responsible practices within the commodity sector. While it presents unique challenges, it has the potential to drive positive change in areas critical to the well-being of society and the environment while delivering financial returns. Due diligence, transparency, and alignment with well-defined impact objectives are essential for successful impact investing in commodities.

Chapter 9: Technology in Commodity Trading

Technological Advancements in Trading Platforms

Technology has transformed commodity trading, making it more efficient, accessible, and responsive to market dynamics. Here are some of the key technological advancements in commodity trading platforms:

a. Electronic Trading:

⟐ **Transition from Open-Outcry to Electronic Trading:** Many commodity markets have shifted from open-outcry trading floors to electronic trading platforms. This transition has led to faster order execution, reduced trading costs, and improved transparency.

⟐ **High-Frequency Trading (HFT):** High-frequency trading firms use advanced algorithms and technology to execute trades at extremely high speeds, often in microseconds. HFT has increased market liquidity and provided market makers with more efficient tools.

b. Online Trading Platforms:

⟐ **Web-Based Trading:** Online trading platforms allow traders to access commodity markets via web browsers. These platforms offer real-time market data, charting tools, and order execution capabilities.

⟐ **Mobile Trading Apps:** Mobile apps have made it possible for traders to monitor and execute trades from smartphones and tablets, providing flexibility and accessibility.

c. Algorithmic Trading:

◈ **Algorithmic Trading:** Algorithms are used to automate trading strategies, enabling traders to execute orders based on predefined criteria, such as price movements or technical indicators. This technology has increased trading efficiency and reduced the impact of human emotions on trading decisions.

◈ **Machine Learning and AI:** Machine learning and artificial intelligence are applied to analyze vast amounts of data and identify trading opportunities, risk management strategies, and market trends.

d. Risk Management Systems:

◈ **Risk Analytics:** Advanced risk management systems use quantitative models to assess and manage market, credit, and operational risks associated with commodity trading.

e. Trade Surveillance and Compliance:

◈ **Trade Surveillance Tools:** Technology is employed for trade surveillance to detect and prevent market manipulation, fraud, and insider trading. Automated surveillance systems analyze trading patterns and behaviors in real time.

◈ **Compliance Software:** Trading firms use compliance software to ensure that they adhere to regulatory requirements and reporting obligations.

f. Data Analytics and Big Data:

◈ **Big Data Analysis:** Commodity traders utilize big data analytics to process and analyze vast amounts of market data, improving decision-making and risk assessment.

◈ **Predictive Analytics:** Predictive analytics models forecast future price movements and trends, helping traders make informed trading decisions.

g. Blockchain and Distributed Ledger Technology (DLT):

◈ **Blockchain for Supply Chain Management:** In commodities like agriculture, blockchain is used to enhance supply chain transparency and traceability, reducing fraud and ensuring product quality.

◈ **Smart Contracts:** Smart contracts on blockchain platforms enable automated and secure execution of trade agreements, reducing the need for intermediaries and enhancing trust.

h. Real-Time Market Data:

◈ **Market Data Feeds:** Real-time market data feeds provide traders with up-to-the-minute information on prices, supply and demand, news, and geopolitical events.

i. Cloud Computing:

◈ **Cloud-Based Trading:** Cloud computing allows traders to access trading platforms and data from anywhere with an internet connection, facilitating scalability and reducing infrastructure costs.

j. Cybersecurity Measures:

◈ **Cybersecurity Tools:** Commodity trading firms invest in robust cybersecurity measures to protect trading systems and sensitive data from cyber threats.

k. Environmental, Social, and Governance (ESG) Data:

◈ **ESG Integration:** Technology is used to gather, analyze, and incorporate ESG data into trading strategies, aligning investments with sustainability goals.

These technological advancements have reshaped the commodity trading landscape, providing traders with powerful tools to analyze markets, manage risks, and make informed decisions. However, they have also introduced new challenges, such as cybersecurity threats and the need for continuous adaptation to evolving technologies and regulations. As technology continues to advance, commodity trading platforms will likely become even more sophisticated and integrated with other financial markets.

Data analytics and artificial intelligence (AI) have revolutionized commodity trading by providing traders with powerful tools to analyze vast amounts of data, identify trading opportunities, and manage risks more effectively. Here's an overview of how data analytics and AI are used in commodity trading:

1. Market Data Analysis:

◈ **Real-Time Market Data:** Traders use AI and data analytics to process real-time market data, including price feeds, order book data, and news updates, to identify trends and anomalies.

◈ **Pattern Recognition:** Machine learning algorithms can recognize patterns and trends in historical price data, helping traders make informed decisions about entry and exit points.

2. Predictive Analytics:

◈ **Price Forecasting:** AI models are used to forecast future commodity prices based on historical data, market sentiment, and other relevant factors. These forecasts help traders make trading decisions.

◈ **Supply and Demand Analysis:** Predictive analytics can assess supply and demand dynamics, helping traders anticipate price movements due to changing market fundamentals.

3. Risk Management:

◈ **Portfolio Risk Assessment:** AI-driven risk models evaluate portfolio exposure and potential losses under different market conditions, allowing traders to implement risk management strategies effectively.

◈ **Credit Risk Analysis:** Data analytics are used to assess the credit risk associated with counterparties, ensuring that trading partners are financially stable.

4. Algorithmic Trading:

◈ **Algorithmic Strategies:** Traders deploy AI-driven algorithms to execute trades automatically based on predefined criteria. These algorithms can adapt to changing market conditions and execute trades at high speeds.

◈ **Market Microstructure Analysis:** AI models analyze market microstructure data, including order flow and liquidity, to optimize trading strategies and execution.

5. Sentiment Analysis:

◈ **Social Media and News Monitoring:** AI tools analyze social media posts and news articles to gauge market sentiment and identify potential market-moving events.

◈ **Natural Language Processing (NLP):** NLP techniques process text data to extract insights about market sentiment and news sentiment.

6. Trade Surveillance:

◈ **Anomaly Detection:** AI-powered surveillance systems identify irregular trading patterns and potential market manipulation, enhancing compliance and risk management.

7. Supply Chain Traceability:

◈ **Blockchain and DLT:** Blockchain technology is used to trace the origin and movement of commodities in the supply chain. AI can analyze this data for transparency and authenticity, helping ensure ethical sourcing.

8. Trading Strategy Optimization:

◈ **Reinforcement Learning:** AI agents learn and optimize trading strategies through reinforcement learning, adapting to changing market conditions.

9. Portfolio Management:

◈ **Portfolio Optimization:** AI-driven portfolio management tools help traders allocate assets efficiently to achieve specific risk-return profiles.

10. ESG Integration:

◈ **ESG Data Analysis:** Data analytics and AI incorporate environmental, social, and governance (ESG) data into trading strategies, aligning investments with sustainability goals.

While data analytics and AI offer significant advantages in commodity trading, there are also challenges, including data quality and the need for robust cybersecurity measures. Additionally, the use of AI in trading raises ethical and regulatory questions related to algorithmic trading and market manipulation.

As technology continues to advance, the role of data analytics and AI in commodity trading will likely expand, providing traders with increasingly sophisticated tools for decision-making, risk management, and achieving both financial and sustainability goals.

Blockchain technology has gained significant attention for its ability to enhance supply chain transparency in commodity trading and various industries. It provides an immutable and transparent ledger that records transactions and data across a network of participants, ensuring data integrity and traceability. Here's how blockchain contributes to supply chain transparency in commodity trading:

1. Traceability and Provenance:

◈ **End-to-End Visibility:** Blockchain enables the recording of every transaction or event in the supply chain, from production to distribution. Each participant along the supply chain can access this information, creating complete visibility.

◈ **Product Origin:** Consumers and stakeholders can trace the origin of commodities, such as agricultural products, minerals, and energy resources. This transparency helps ensure ethical sourcing and authenticity.

2. Tamper-Resistant Records:

◈ **Immutable Records:** Once data is recorded on the blockchain, it cannot be altered or deleted without consensus from network participants. This immutability ensures data integrity and prevents fraudulent activities.

3. Smart Contracts:

◈ **Automated Agreements:** Smart contracts are self-executing agreements with predefined conditions. In commodity trading, they can automate various aspects, such as payment upon delivery confirmation, reducing the risk of contract disputes and fraud.

4. Ethical and Sustainable Practices:

◈ **Proof of Compliance:** Blockchain can provide proof of adherence to ethical and sustainable practices, such as fair labor conditions, environmental protection, and responsible sourcing. This transparency is crucial for demonstrating compliance with industry standards and regulations.

5. Supply Chain Efficiency:

◈ **Reduced Delays and Errors:** Blockchain streamlines supply chain processes by reducing paperwork, manual data entry, and reconciliation efforts. This efficiency minimizes delays and errors in commodity trading.

6. Counterparty Verification:

◈ **Verification of Trading Partners:** Participants in the supply chain can verify the authenticity and legitimacy of their trading partners, reducing the risk of trading with unreliable or fraudulent entities.

7. Quality Control:

◈ **Quality Assurance:** Blockchain can record quality control data, such as inspections, certifications, and quality tests, ensuring that commodities meet specified standards.

8. Real-Time Updates:

◈ **Real-Time Tracking:** Participants can track the movement and status of commodities in real time. This capability helps optimize logistics, reduce waste, and respond promptly to supply chain disruptions.

9. Food Safety:

◈ **Food Traceability:** In the agricultural sector, blockchain enhances food safety by providing a transparent record of a product's journey from farm to table. It facilitates rapid recalls in case of contamination or safety issues.

10. Sustainability Initiatives:

◈ **Carbon Tracking:** Blockchain can be used to track carbon emissions throughout the supply chain, supporting sustainability initiatives and carbon footprint reduction.

11. Regulatory Compliance:

◈ **Regulatory Reporting:** Blockchain simplifies the reporting of compliance with regulatory requirements related to commodities, reducing administrative burdens.

12. Consumer Trust:

◈ **Consumer Confidence:** Increased transparency fosters consumer trust, as consumers can access detailed information about the products they purchase, including their origin and quality.

While blockchain technology offers numerous advantages for supply chain transparency in commodity trading, its implementation requires collaboration among industry stakeholders and adherence to common standards. Additionally, data privacy and security considerations must be addressed to protect sensitive supply chain information. As blockchain continues to evolve, it has the potential to revolutionize how commodities are traded and tracked, promoting responsible and ethical practices across global supply chains.

Cybersecurity is a critical concern in commodity trading due to the increasing reliance on digital technologies and the potential for cyber threats to disrupt trading operations, compromise sensitive data, and cause financial losses. Here's an overview of cybersecurity in commodity trading:

1. Cyber Threat Landscape:

◈ **Cyberattacks:** Commodity trading firms face various cyber threats, including ransomware attacks, phishing attempts, distributed denial of service (DDoS) attacks, and data breaches.

◈ **Insider Threats:** Insider threats can come from employees, contractors, or other trusted individuals with access to trading systems and sensitive data.

2. Key Cybersecurity Measures:

◈ **Network Security:** Implement robust network security measures, including firewalls, intrusion detection systems, and encryption, to protect against unauthorized access and data breaches.

◈ **Endpoint Security:** Secure all endpoints (devices) used in commodity trading with antivirus software, regular updates, and intrusion detection.

◈ **Authentication and Access Control:** Enforce strong authentication methods, such as multi-factor authentication (MFA), and restrict access to sensitive systems based on job roles and responsibilities.

◈ **Data Encryption:** Encrypt sensitive data both in transit and at rest to safeguard it from interception and theft.

◈ **Regular Updates and Patch Management:** Keep software, operating systems, and applications up to date with security patches to address known vulnerabilities.

3. Secure Trading Systems:

◈ **Secure APIs:** Ensure that application programming interfaces (APIs) used for trading platforms are secure and protected against attacks.

◈ **Secure Coding Practices:** Develop and maintain trading applications using secure coding practices to minimize vulnerabilities.

◈ **Vendor Security:** Assess the security of third-party trading systems and services, including those offered by trading platforms and technology providers.

4. Employee Training and Awareness:

◈ **Cybersecurity Training:** Provide training to employees on cybersecurity best practices, including how to recognize phishing attempts and how to respond to security incidents.

◈ **Awareness Programs:** Foster a culture of cybersecurity awareness and encourage employees to report any suspicious activities promptly.

5. Incident Response Plan:

◈ **Develop an Incident Response Plan (IRP):** Establish a comprehensive IRP that outlines the steps to take in the event of a cyber incident, including containment, eradication, recovery, and communication procedures.

◈ **Regular Testing:** Periodically test the IRP through simulations and tabletop exercises to ensure that staff can effectively respond to cyber incidents.

6. Data Privacy and Compliance:

◈ **Compliance with Regulations:** Commodity trading firms must comply with data protection regulations, such as GDPR or CCPA, and industry-specific compliance standards.

◈ **Data Minimization:** Limit the amount of personal and sensitive data collected and stored, reducing the potential impact of data breaches.

7. Vendor Risk Management:

◈ **Vendor Assessment:** Evaluate the cybersecurity practices of third-party vendors and assess their potential impact on your organization's security posture.

◈ **Contractual Safeguards:** Include cybersecurity requirements and contractual safeguards in vendor agreements to mitigate risks.

8. Continuous Monitoring:

◈ **Security Monitoring:** Implement continuous monitoring of network traffic, system logs, and user activities to detect and respond to security incidents in real time.

9. Cyber Insurance:

◈ **Cyber Insurance Policies:** Consider purchasing cyber insurance to mitigate financial losses and liabilities associated with cyberattacks and data breaches.

10. Regulatory Compliance:

◈ **Regulatory Requirements:** Commodity trading firms must adhere to cybersecurity regulations and reporting requirements specific to their jurisdiction and industry.

Cybersecurity is an ongoing effort that requires constant vigilance and adaptation to evolving threats. It is crucial for commodity trading firms to prioritize cybersecurity as an integral part of their business operations to safeguard their assets, protect customer data, and maintain the integrity of financial markets. Regular security audits, risk assessments, and employee training are essential components of a robust cybersecurity strategy in commodity trading.

Chapter 10: The Future of Commodity Trading

Emerging Trends in Commodity Markets

Commodity markets are constantly evolving, driven by changes in technology, regulation, consumer preferences, and global economic conditions. Here are some emerging trends that are likely to shape the future of commodity trading:

a. Digitalization and Blockchain:

◈ **Blockchain Integration:** The use of blockchain technology for supply chain transparency and smart contracts is expected to continue growing, enhancing trust and efficiency in commodity trading.

◈ **Digital Marketplaces:** Digital platforms and marketplaces that connect buyers and sellers directly are gaining traction, reducing the need for intermediaries.

b. Sustainability and ESG Focus:

◈ **ESG Integration:** Environmental, Social, and Governance (ESG) considerations are becoming central to commodity trading decisions, with investors and consumers seeking sustainable and responsible products.

◈ **Carbon Trading:** Carbon emissions trading and carbon offset markets are expected to expand as efforts to combat climate change intensify.

c. Renewable Energy Commodities:

◈ **Renewable Energy Credits (RECs):** Trading in RECs is growing as renewable energy sources, such as wind and solar, become more prevalent in the energy mix.

◈ **Hydrogen Trading:** As interest in green hydrogen production grows, trading in hydrogen and related commodities is expected to develop.

d. Artificial Intelligence and Data Analytics:

◈ **AI-Driven Trading:** The use of artificial intelligence and machine learning for algorithmic trading, predictive analytics, and risk management will continue to evolve.

◈ **Big Data Insights:** Big data analytics will provide deeper insights into market dynamics, helping traders make more informed decisions.

e. Regulatory Changes:

◈ **Global Regulations:** Ongoing changes in global regulations, including MiFID II, Dodd-Frank, and EMIR, will impact commodity markets, requiring market participants to adapt to new reporting and compliance requirements.

◈ **Sustainable Finance Regulations:** Increasing regulation around sustainable finance and ESG disclosure will influence commodity trading practices.

f. Energy Transition:

◈ **Transition to Clean Energy:** As the world transitions to cleaner energy sources, traditional fossil fuel markets may decline, while markets for renewable energy commodities and energy storage materials will expand.

g. Decentralized Finance (DeFi):

◈ **DeFi Platforms:** Decentralized finance platforms are beginning to offer commodity trading services, challenging traditional financial intermediaries.

h. Geopolitical Factors:

◈ **Geopolitical Tensions:** Geopolitical events and trade disputes can impact commodity markets, leading to volatility and supply chain disruptions.

i. Technological Innovation:

◈ **Quantum Computing:** The development of quantum computing has the potential to revolutionize risk modeling and optimization in commodity trading.

◈ **Internet of Things (IoT):** IoT devices that monitor commodity production and logistics will provide real-time data to improve decision-making.

j. Trade Finance Innovation:

◈ **Blockchain-Based Trade Finance:** Trade finance solutions based on blockchain technology can streamline financing processes in commodity trading.

k. Circular Economy:

◈ **Recycling and Reuse:** Increasing emphasis on recycling and the circular economy will impact commodity markets by changing the demand for raw materials.

The future of commodity trading will be shaped by a combination of technological advancements, sustainability imperatives, regulatory changes, and shifting market dynamics. Traders and market participants must remain agile and adaptable to thrive in this evolving landscape. As sustainability and responsible trading practices gain prominence, commodities will continue to play a critical role in meeting global economic and environmental challenges.

Emerging markets play a crucial and increasingly prominent role in commodity trading due to their growing economies, expanding populations, and significant natural resource reserves. Here's an overview of the role of emerging markets in commodity trading:

1. Rising Demand:

◈ **Population Growth:** Emerging markets often have rapidly growing populations, leading to increased demand for essential commodities like food, energy, and minerals.

◈ **Urbanization:** As urbanization continues in emerging markets, there is a greater need for construction materials, energy for infrastructure development, and commodities to support urban lifestyles.

2. Natural Resource Richness:

◈ **Resource Abundance:** Many emerging markets are rich in natural resources, including oil, minerals, metals, and agricultural land. This makes them major suppliers in global commodity markets.

◈ **Energy Production:** Several emerging markets are among the world's leading energy producers, contributing significantly to global oil and gas markets.

3. Agricultural Commodities:

◈ **Agricultural Exports:** Emerging markets often export agricultural products like grains, coffee, and tropical fruits to meet global demand.

◈ **Agribusiness:** The expansion of agribusiness and modern farming practices in emerging markets has increased their role in global agricultural commodity trading.

4. Metals and Minerals:

◈ **Mining Operations:** Emerging markets host substantial mining operations, producing minerals like iron ore, copper, and aluminum, which are vital for industrial production worldwide.

◈ **Technology Metals:** Some emerging markets are key suppliers of technology metals such as rare earth elements and lithium, which are critical for electronics and renewable energy technologies.

5. Energy Commodities:

◈ **Oil and Gas:** Several emerging markets are major exporters of oil and natural gas, contributing significantly to global energy markets.

◈ **Renewable Energy:** Some emerging markets are investing in renewable energy projects and trading renewable energy certificates, impacting the energy mix and trading dynamics.

6. Infrastructure Development:

◈ **Infrastructure Needs:** Emerging markets require substantial infrastructure development, leading to increased demand for commodities like steel, cement, and construction materials.

◈ **Commodities in Infrastructure:** Infrastructure projects, such as roads, bridges, and buildings, rely on commodities like steel, copper, and cement.

7. Investment Opportunities:

◈ **Investor Interest:** Emerging markets offer attractive investment opportunities in commodities, attracting foreign investment and enhancing their position in global trading.

8. Supply Chain Diversification:

◈ **Diversified Supply Chains:** Companies seeking to diversify their supply chains often look to emerging markets as alternative sourcing locations for commodities.

9. Environmental and Sustainability Factors:

◈ **Sustainable Practices:** Emerging markets are increasingly focusing on sustainable commodity production and are adopting practices that meet global environmental standards.

◈ **Carbon Markets:** Some emerging markets are exploring carbon trading and emissions reduction initiatives.

10. Geopolitical Influence:

◈ **Geopolitical Factors:** The geopolitical influence of emerging market countries can impact commodity markets, including oil and natural gas prices and supply chain disruptions.

11. Trade Agreements:

◈ **Bilateral and Multilateral Agreements:** Emerging markets often engage in trade agreements with other countries and regions, affecting the flow of commodities.

12. Regulatory Environment:

◈ **Regulatory Changes:** Emerging markets may implement regulatory changes that impact commodity trading within their borders and globally.

While emerging markets present significant opportunities in commodity trading, they also face challenges such as infrastructure constraints, regulatory uncertainties, and political instability. Additionally, commodity trading in emerging markets can be subject to price volatility, environmental concerns, and ethical considerations.

As emerging markets continue to grow and develop, their role in global commodity trading is expected to expand further. Their influence on commodity prices, supply chain dynamics, and sustainability practices will shape the future of commodity trading on a global scale.

Green commodities and renewable energy sources are becoming increasingly important in commodity trading as the world shifts toward more sustainable and environmentally friendly practices. These commodities play a critical role in addressing climate change and meeting growing energy demands while reducing greenhouse gas emissions. Here's an overview of green commodities and their impact on renewable energy:

1. Renewable Energy Sources:

◈ **Solar Energy:** Solar panels capture energy from the sun's rays and convert it into electricity. Solar farms and rooftop solar installations are common sources of renewable energy.

◈ **Wind Energy:** Wind turbines generate electricity as the kinetic energy from wind is converted into rotational motion. Wind farms are established to harness this energy.

◈ **Hydropower:** Energy is generated by the flow of water, often from rivers or dams, turning turbines and producing electricity.

◈ **Biomass Energy:** Biomass, such as organic materials and agricultural waste, can be burned to produce heat or electricity.

◈ **Geothermal Energy:** This involves tapping into the Earth's internal heat to generate electricity and provide heating.

2. Green Commodities Associated with Renewable Energy:

◈ **Renewable Energy Certificates (RECs):** RECs represent the environmental attributes of one megawatt-hour of electricity generated from renewable sources. They can be traded to demonstrate the use of renewable energy and meet sustainability goals.

◈ **Battery Metals:** Commodities like lithium, cobalt, and nickel are essential for battery production in renewable energy storage systems, such as lithium-ion batteries used in electric vehicles and energy storage.

◈ **Biofuels:** Biofuels, including ethanol and biodiesel, are derived from renewable sources like corn, sugarcane, and algae. They are used as alternatives to traditional fossil fuels in transportation and heating.

◈ **Carbon Credits:** These credits represent a reduction in greenhouse gas emissions, often generated by renewable energy projects. They can be traded in carbon markets to offset emissions.

◈ **Green Hydrogen:** Hydrogen produced using renewable energy sources, known as green hydrogen, is gaining attention as a potential clean fuel for various industries, including transportation and energy production.

3. Impact on Commodity Trading:

◈ **Market Growth:** The demand for green commodities associated with renewable energy is growing as countries and companies seek to reduce their carbon footprints and transition to cleaner energy sources.

◈ **Price Volatility:** Price dynamics for some green commodities, such as lithium, can be influenced by factors like technological advancements, government policies, and supply chain fluctuations.

◈ **Global Supply Chains:** The global supply chains for green commodities are becoming increasingly complex as production and distribution networks expand to meet growing demand.

◈ **Technological Innovation:** Advances in renewable energy technologies, including energy storage and grid integration, impact the supply and demand for related commodities.

4. Sustainability and Environmental Impact:

◈ **Environmental Benefits:** Green commodities contribute to reducing greenhouse gas emissions, mitigating the effects of climate change, and preserving natural resources.

◈ **Ethical Sourcing:** The responsible sourcing of green commodities is crucial to ensure that environmental and social standards are upheld throughout their production.

5. Policy and Regulation:

◈ **Government Incentives:** Government policies and incentives, such as renewable energy targets and subsidies, can significantly influence the production and trading of green commodities.

◈ **Carbon Markets:** The establishment of carbon markets and emissions trading systems can drive demand for carbon credits, encouraging investment in renewable energy projects.

6. Investor Interest:

◈ **Sustainable Investments:** Investors are increasingly interested in green commodities and renewable energy projects as part of their sustainable and responsible investment strategies.

◈ **ESG Considerations:** Environmental, Social, and Governance (ESG) criteria play a significant role in investment decisions related to green commodities and renewable energy.

Green commodities and renewable energy are poised to transform the energy landscape and commodity trading markets. As global efforts to combat climate change intensify, the role of these commodities in addressing environmental challenges and achieving sustainability goals will continue to grow, making them a pivotal part of the future of commodity trading.

The future of commodity trading holds both challenges and opportunities as markets evolve, technologies advance, and global dynamics change. Here's a closer look at some of the key challenges and opportunities that commodity trading will likely face:

Challenges:

1. **Climate Change and ESG Compliance:**

◈ *Challenge:* Commodity trading faces increasing scrutiny regarding its environmental impact and adherence to Environmental, Social, and Governance (ESG) standards. Climate change regulations and sustainability expectations may pose challenges for certain commodities, especially those associated with high carbon emissions.

◈ *Opportunity:* Meeting ESG standards and adopting sustainable practices can open doors to new markets, attract responsible investors, and enhance reputation.

2. **Technological Complexity:**

⟐ *Challenge:* Rapid technological advancements bring complexity to commodity trading, including cybersecurity risks, the need for skilled data analysts, and the potential for algorithmic trading errors.

⟐ *Opportunity:* Effective use of technology can increase efficiency, reduce costs, and provide valuable insights into market trends and risk management.

3. **Geopolitical Uncertainty:**

⟐ *Challenge:* Geopolitical tensions and trade disputes can disrupt supply chains and create market volatility, affecting commodity prices.

⟐ *Opportunity:* Diversifying supply chains and developing contingency plans can mitigate geopolitical risks.

4. **Regulatory Changes:**

⟐ *Challenge:* Evolving regulations, such as MiFID II and Dodd-Frank, can impact trading practices and compliance requirements.

⟐ *Opportunity:* Staying informed about regulatory changes and adapting to new reporting and compliance standards can enhance market integrity and reduce legal risks.

5. **Commodity Price Volatility:**

⟐ *Challenge:* Commodity prices can be highly volatile, influenced by factors like weather events, geopolitical crises, and supply-demand imbalances.

⟐ *Opportunity:* Price volatility creates trading opportunities, and effective risk management strategies can mitigate potential losses.

6. **Sustainable Practices:**

◈ *Challenge:* Ensuring ethical sourcing, promoting sustainable practices, and managing supply chain transparency can be complex and resource-intensive.

◈ *Opportunity:* Meeting sustainability goals can attract responsible consumers and investors, fostering long-term business growth.

Opportunities:

1. **Green Commodities and Renewable Energy:**

◈ *Opportunity:* The transition to green commodities and renewable energy sources presents significant opportunities for traders to participate in the growing demand for sustainable products and technologies.

2. **Technology Integration:**

◈ *Opportunity:* Leveraging advanced technologies such as blockchain, AI, and big data analytics can enhance trading efficiency, transparency, and decision-making capabilities.

3. **Market Diversification:**

◈ *Opportunity:* Exploring emerging markets and diversifying commodity portfolios can reduce risk and open up new trading opportunities.

4. **Sustainable Finance:**

◈ *Opportunity:* Sustainable finance instruments, including green bonds and impact investing, provide avenues for traders to align investments with ESG goals.

5. **Supply Chain Innovation:**

◈ *Opportunity:* Embracing supply chain innovations like blockchain and IoT can improve traceability, reduce costs, and enhance trust throughout the supply chain.

6. **Geographical Expansion:**

◈ *Opportunity:* Expanding trading activities into regions with growing economies and resource-rich reserves can lead to increased market presence and revenue opportunities.

7. **Carbon Markets:**

◈ *Opportunity:* Participating in carbon markets and trading carbon credits can diversify trading portfolios and align with carbon reduction goals.

8. **Sustainability Reporting:**

◈ *Opportunity:* Providing transparent sustainability reporting can build trust with stakeholders and attract responsible investors.

The future of commodity trading will require adaptability, innovation, and a strong commitment to sustainability and responsible practices. While challenges such as regulatory changes and market volatility persist, the opportunities presented by green commodities, technology integration, and evolving market dynamics can drive growth and success in the commodity trading sector. Traders and market participants who proactively address these challenges and seize opportunities stand to thrive in the evolving landscape of commodity trading.

Don't miss out!

Visit the website below and you can sign up to receive emails whenever Alex Thompson publishes a new book. There's no charge and no obligation.

https://books2read.com/r/B-A-FEPY-VJVOC

BOOKS 2 READ

Connecting independent readers to independent writers.

Also by Alex Thompson

Alex on Finance

Financial Freedom Roadmap - Achieving Early Retirement through the FIRE Movement

The Art of Strategic Innovation

Beyond Cash - The Evolution of Digital Payment Systems and the Future of Money

Preserving Wealth in Inflationary Times - Strategies for Protecting Your Financial Future

Standalone

Side Hustle Success: Unlocking Your Entrepreneurial Potential

Side Hustle Success: The Ultimate Guide to Passive and Financial Freedom

Mastering the Markets: Advanced Trading Strategies for Success and Ethical Trading Practices

Financial Fortitude

Mastering the Art of Upselling

The Financial Bullet Blueprint

Investing Demystified: A Beginner's Guide to Building Wealth in the Stock Market

Real Estate Riches: Building Wealth through Property Investment

How To Succeed as a Freelancer

Navigating Complex Waters: Advanced Strategies in Portfolio Management
Behavioral Finance and Investor Psychology
Leading with Empathy: Harnessing Emotional Intelligence for Effective Leadership
Financial Independence
Thriving Within Your Means: A Guide to Affordable Living
Algorithmic Trading: Navigating the Digital Frontier
Navigating Alternative Investments
Navigating the Behavioral Finance Landscape
Unlocking the Power of Derivatives
Mastering International Finance
Quantitative Finance and Risk Modeling
Sustainable and ESG Investing
Derivatives Dynamics: Navigating Risk and Innovation
Options Mastery: Navigating the Financial Frontier
Portfolio Mastery: Navigating the Financial Art and Science
Ethics in Hedge Funds: Navigating the Moral Compass of Finance
Structured Finance: Navigating Innovation, Sustainability and Ethics
Commodity Trading: Navigating Markets, Sustainability, and Innovation
Ethical Valuation: Navigating the Future of Startup Investments
Navigating Financial Risk: Strategies for a Dynamic World

www.ingramcontent.com/pod-product-compliance
Lightning Source LLC
LaVergne TN
LVHW022057200926
848481LV00003B/963
* 9 7 9 8 2 2 3 5 5 9 6 1 0 *